June,

Thanks for reading.
Hope you enjoy
the stories.

Blake Sebring

FEATURES IN FAITH

EVERYDAY PEOPLE'S EXPERIENCES WITH GOD

Blake Sebring

Foreword by Don Wharton
Cover Design by Angel Knuth
Edited by Melody Schmitt Foreman

DEDICATION

Thank you to everyone featured in this book for trusting me and allowing me to tell your very personal stories. You have been a blessing to me and hopefully to many more through this book.

For Bethlehem Lutheran Church
School, sanctuary, home

VERSE

"As each has received a gift, use it to serve one another, as good stewards of God's varied grace." 1 Peter 4:10

ALSO BY BLAKE SEBRING

Tales of the Komets
Legends of the Komets
Live from Radio Rinkside: The Bob Chase Story
The Biggest Mistake I Never Made (with Lloy Ball)
The Lake Effect
Homecoming Game
Fort Wayne Sports History
Lethal Ghost
On to The Show: Fort Wayne's lasting impact on the NHL
   and the hockey world

FOREWORD

Blake Sebring and I take time to talk over lunch every so often when I'm in town and he has a break in his schedule. It doesn't happen as often as we'd like, but when we do get together, the conversation stays lively and picturesque. You see, we're both storytellers. We try to stay away from talking about politics, because we have some opposite views and we each hold on to those views passionately. Besides, we have enough to talk about because we each like all aspects of sports and we appreciate the interesting lives of people we've met along the way. And those two subjects can keep us busy for hours.

The other subject we don't shy away from is living out our faith in God. We both believe in exercising our faith daily. Some days, we come off as superstars, but most days, we're sinners in need of God's grace — badly in need.

Blake goes to the same church I grew up in, Bethlehem Lutheran on the south side of Fort Wayne (Indiana). He still enjoys the traditional liturgical style of worship, while I lean toward the more contemporary style. However, we each connect with the "realness" of Jesus and the adventure of following Him.

We've all heard that "God works in mysterious ways." More often, though, we see God working in the unforeseen events that happen to common people who demonstrate courage they never knew they had, wisdom beyond their years, and love that overflows to people who need it most.

Blake Sebring has captured a myriad of these stories in his book "Features in Faith" that illustrate faith in the flesh — God working through ordinary people in extraordinary ways. These true stories are sure to inspire and encourage readers to recognize the unexpected and remarkable opportunities God gives each of us to exercise our own faith in our daily lives.

Don Wharton • July 6, 2018

INTRODUCTION

As a writer, I love to tell people's stories about courage, redemption, persistence and overcoming challenges. As a Christian, I realize a lot of those things can only happen through faith.

So when I come across a person with a story I want to tell, not always but often I'll ask them if faith played a factor in it. Though some may look at me oddly and say it did not, sometimes they say faith was a huge part of their experience, and they are happy to talk about it.

When I helped Bob Chase and Lloy Ball write their biographies, I encouraged each to include a chapter about his faith. I knew both were strong Christians, but I also couldn't remember reading many biographies where faith was a significant topic. If faith is such a large part of your life, I argued, shouldn't it be included in your story?

Both eagerly agreed.

Bob talked about getting ready for his quadruple bypass surgery in 1998 and how a feeling of serenity and relaxation had come over him while he was waiting on the gurney outside the operating room. His daughter Karin had just put out a prayer request among her friends.

"Prayer was working for me," Bob said. "I could feel it. It was an amazing feeling. I've never had a feeling like that before or again in my life. It was just unreal. I was at peace with the world completely."

Of course, Bob survived the surgery and recovered to live almost 20 more years.

"I still think that what helped me recover so quickly was faith again. I never had any thought in my mind at any point and time that I wasn't coming back again and I wasn't going to be OK. It was going to work out perfectly, because I knew all the people who were my doctors. I had total faith in my doctor and faith in God, and that was what did it."

Lloy Ball was raised in a Christian family and has built his own with his wife, Sarah. Considering all the places in the world he has lived and worked throughout his volleyball career, he always has an interesting perspective.

"I think God is the reason why I have the life I have," he said after winning a 2008 Olympic gold medal. "I also believe it's our hard work together, but that He has guided us in that direction. I'm not a Born-Again (Christian). We have Mormons on the national team, we have Born-Agains, we have Catholics, we have Jews, we have everybody, and I'm fine with all of it. I'm fine with Muslims, I'm fine with Hindu. If you look at any religion, the principles are the same, and it's the fundamentalists and other people who change that. It's that there is a God, he made the world, he sent a son who died and rose to save us. As long as you believe that, the rest is just something to argue about on Sunday.

"The perspective I talk to my mom and dad about is that I have seen so much. How can a billion Chinese be condemned to hell? It's not possible, I don't think. There has to be some kind of connection with all of these religions. I've lived in Italy where it is 99 percent Catholic, I've lived in Greece where it's Greek Orthodox, I've lived in Russia where it's Russian Orthodox. I don't have enough blinders on to condemn all those people. I think God, Muhammad, Allah, whatever you want to call him, is much more compassionate than we are. I think he lets some things slide as long as you're not a nut bag like some of these fundamentalists are nowadays. As long as you follow a couple of principles, I think you are good to go."

It was fascinating to hear their perspectives, and that encouraged me to continue asking other interview subjects what their thoughts were about faith, which is where the stories in this book come from. We've become such a secular world that we often don't ask or talk about religion and faith outside of our churches, but those are still themes and ideas I enjoy exploring with people in my stories.

There have been many times over the years when I have woken in the morning with the idea — from God, I believe — that I'm supposed to go talk to specific individuals. It's gotten to the point where I don't question these feelings or hesitate, I just go. When I meet the person, it usually becomes clear to me pretty quickly why I've been directed there. I like to refer to these situations as taps on the shoulder from God.

I may find out the reason why I was directed to write a particular story, though sometimes not for a long time. I accept nonetheless that there was a distinct purpose.

As an example, one day I awoke with the need to go see the Fort Wayne Komets' assistant equipment manager, Jack Prindle. I found out he was a Vietnam War veteran who had come home and gotten married, become an alcoholic, undergone shock therapy, gotten divorced, become homeless, been abandoned in Las Vegas by a buddy, and come home to undergo more shock therapy. (Jack's full story is included in this collection.)

Anyway, about two years after the 2005 story was published

in The (Fort Wayne) News-Sentinel, I received a letter from a woman who identified herself as Jack's sister-in-law. She wanted my help in contacting Jack, because he and his brother had not spoken in almost 50 years, and it was time for them to repair their relationship. That's exactly what happened.

Talk about shivers!

There have been a few times over the years when I've discovered the reason for talking to someone much later, and every once in a while, I'll come in contact with a subject who'll tell me how one of my stories affected their life. That's the ultimate tap on the shoulder.

So fast-forward to a weekend in early June 2018 when I was excited to research and tell a pair of stories. One was about Alissa Jagger, who three years after becoming paralyzed, walked across the stage to receive her high school diploma. The other was about how North Manchester, Ind., was rallying around miracle baby Finley "Fierce" Terflinger, an 8-month-old girl with an 8-centimeter-by-8-centimeter tumor in her chest that had disappeared. I was sitting in church on the Saturday night before the interviews when I caught a line in Pastor Jeff Geisler's readings that included something about God's support in our endeavors. That's when I knew I was supposed to compile the stories for this book.

I didn't argue.

So I looked over my work from the past 30 years and highlighted the stories that affected me the most. If you've ever wondered how God works in practical ways in today's world, these are some wonderful testimonies. They come from people and events in northeast Indiana, but they could happen anywhere.

Consider the location Anytown, U.S.A. They are broken into short stories, as published in print and online, and as such are suited well for coffee table or daily devotional-style reading. Hopefully, they will provide real-world examples to help answer a few of your questions. And if you find inspiration in the pages along the way, well … maybe you're getting your own tap on the shoulder.

Blake Sebring
June 15, 2018

Editor's note: The stories in this compilation are written from the time perspective of their publication date, which is included with each chapter.

CHAPTER 1
As hours ticked away,
Leah Smith always believed
Published June 25, 2013, in The News-Sentinel

When she was born March 28, 1991, Leah Smith weighed 8 pounds and one-half ounce, and she was 21 inches long, but she immediately exhibited breathing problems and was placed under incubation lights. She needed a heart transplant and received one 11 days later.

Smith became a spokesperson for children's medical issues, an online radio personality, a figure skater and an inspiration to many others as a volunteer for the Indiana Organ Procurement Organization.

"There's always a need for organs and to get awareness out so other people can have a chance," she said when she was 17.

No one said how close Smith was to dying on June 18, 2013, but it was the unspoken threat for doctors, nurses and family members. Everyone sensed it, including Smith.

The hope for her initial transplant was to keep her alive for at least 10 years, and after 22 years, her heart was finally wearing out. She'd been living in Indianapolis off and on since Dec. 10, 2012, when she suffered a heart attack. A second one Feb. 27 left her hospitalized until April 10, when she was forced to continue treatment as an outpatient.

After her heart was further distressed, she was readmitted May 20 to Methodist Hospital, where she'd been fighting to lose weight and undergo treatment to qualify for national donor lists. Because of her heart problems, Smith had been gaining weight, and her body mass index had reached well above the maximum of 35 to qualify for donor lists.

Eating a very low-calorie, low-sodium diet, Smith lost 38 pounds, but she was exhausted. She also was subjected to constant plasmapheresis treatments, which essentially strain her blood for harmful antigens. A balloon pump was installed to help her heart continue beating.

After the pump had to be repositioned and replaced, doctors knew Smith was in trouble and needed help. There were problems with her blood pressure. They were also concerned about her kidneys. One potential treatment was to give her a transfusion, but that would undo all the work they had done to eliminate the antigens, severely limiting her chances for another donor heart.

The doctors felt they needed to do something to help Smith's heart survive. They were considering a VAD (ventricular assist device), but they also knew she needed additional blood to increase her pressure.

"That was a really big blow to what we thought the future would be," her father, Creager Smith, said. "Leah knew she was deteriorating."

When things were looking their worst and the doctors were preparing to do something they knew would hurt Smith's chance for another donor heart, she was the one who kept encouraging everyone else.

"I agree to do this," she said. "Just be aware that as soon as you get me ready to do this, there could be a heart come available."

While the other doctors left to prepare, Dr. Jacqueline O'Donnell, the medical director for the Cardiac Transplant Program at the IU School of Medicine, stayed behind to talk to Smith. Dr. Thomas Wozniak stuck his head into the room and said, "Jackie, I need to see you."

While they were talking in the hall, a nurse came in and removed the blood transfusion bag. Finally, everyone on the surgical team came back into the room.

"Well ...," Dr. Wozniak said.

"You've got a heart," Smith's mother, Joan, said.

"Who told you?" Dr. Wozniak asked.

"No one told me anything," Joan Smith said.

"No, really, who told you?" Dr. Wozniak responded.

"Really?" Joan Smith asked.

"You guys are unreal!" Leah Smith said with a laugh.

Finally, Dr. M. Azam Hadi stepped forward and said, "No, really, there is a heart available."

Here's how close the entire process came to falling apart: First, if any part of the blood transfusion had reached Smith's veins, she would have been taken off the national transplant list and been eligible only for an Indiana donor because new antigens would have been introduced. Second, Methodist's transplant coordinator was talking by phone to another coordinator about taking Smith off the list when the other coordinator said they had a possible heart for her.

Still, the doctors didn't know if the heart would work or when it would arrive. Surgery was originally scheduled for 6 p.m., but it was pushed back to 8 p.m., then 9:15 p.m.

Another problem was finding a heart transplant surgeon. Dr. Mark Turrentine, who had assisted on Smith's initial transplant 22 years earlier, had agreed to lead this operation. Because of the uncertainty of when Smith's surgery would take place, he already had a full slate of surgeries scheduled at Riley Hospital for Children during the time when she would be ready.

Instead, Dr. John Brown, who led the team on the original transplant but who had been in semi-retirement, agreed to take the lead.

Despite all the activity, doctors still didn't know if the new heart would be a match for Smith. They told her they'd prepare for surgery, either to implant the VAD or to give her a transplant, and they would make the decision while she was in the surgical theater on the heart and lung bypass machine.

Doctors also knew the VAD was not really what Smith needed for long-term health. It was a bandage that might give her a few extra days until a new heart could be found, but they knew it would probably only last a short time.

At midnight, the decision was made to accept the new heart, which finally arrived at 2 a.m.

There were still plenty of challenges with the surgery. When Smith received her first transplant, she was 11 days old but her new heart was 9 months old, meaning it was always too big for her chest to comfortably accommodate. It kept bumping against her sternum, creating scar tissue, which doctors now had to deal with.

The surgery was finally completed at about 7 a.m. Wednesday, and Smith arrived in the intensive care unit at about 9 a.m. She stayed on the ventilator for a full day and spent Thursday going in and out of consciousness.

By Friday, she was walking around the unit.

"It's just really remarkable to see the immediate transformation from having her in total heart failure and not able to do anything to now where her heart is fantastic and is working perfectly," her father said.

"Joan and I were talking about it at lunch. You never imagine that lightning would hit once, but twice like this? We are so blessed that she got another heart. We'll continue to always have in mind that there is another family out there that has lost their loved one."

Creager Smith said that if he thought too long about all the things that had to happen for his daughter to continue to live, it would be crippling. As he said, it's weird how the abnormal becomes normal eventually.

"Faith is the greatest imperative," he said. "We absolutely know that God makes miracles. It's interesting once you've really experienced God's miracles to know that sometimes there are little miracles that are hard to perceive and maybe no one knows about them until after the fact. Then there are times when God makes miracles that no one can possibly deny or miss.

"We were praying for God's timing. It's so frustrating to wait, but we knew we were waiting for something horrible to happen to some other family and some other person. That's really hard to deal with."

The Smiths only know that the donor came from out of state. The heart was declined by two other potential recipients before it came to Smith because it was too small.

Doctors continue to watch Leah's kidneys, and she has four drainage tubes to deal with because her body is adjusting to the perfect fit of her new heart. The spaces required for the previous larger heart will have to close up.

Sometime this week, a target date for her return home might be set. As Smith continues to get stronger, her family and doctors hope there will be fewer issues. They are really hoping to experience a little peace for a while.

"Every cardiologist that looks at her tells us they are thrilled with how she is doing because they understood better than us how bad she was doing," Creager Smith said. "They have joy because they know how close she was.

"We prayed for that perfect heart to come in God's way and in his time. Wow, it's obvious that sometimes God appreciates drama."

Maybe, but Leah has been trying to live a calmer life ever since.

"I don't think there ever will be another 'normal life' for me again," she said a few days after the surgery. "My life will consist of constantly trying to give back and tell my story about transplantation to share with the thousands of people still out there needing to make the choice of becoming an organ donor. My life will continue and improve, trying to improve myself and honor my donor with the life I have been newly given.

"I've made it pretty clear that all of this happened by God's grace and his miracles alone. I guess I just want to drive that home, that I only had minutes left on 'Jimmy's' (the first donor) heart, and if God had not provided in the seconds and moments that he did, this would be a different ending to the story. Prayer, through the Team Leah (website) and all the other networks praying for me, is how I am still here today."

CHAPTER 2
Inspirational Paige Eakright looking for a little normal in 2018
Published Dec. 31, 2017, on News-Sentinel.com

The holidays are almost over, and everyone is sitting in traffic, getting last-second shopping completed or maybe trying to do chores around the house that have been put off too long, trying to squeeze things in around a few dozen other appointments. We'd all just like a little bit of normal to return before we forget what it feels like.

But no one wants it more than Paige Eakright. In fact, the Huntington University sophomore can't remember what it feels like or if she'd even recognize it anymore.

Normal. That could be interesting, she thinks.

What's the most inspiring thing you heard of in 2017? It might be Eakright, a 19-year-old Homestead High School graduate and member of the Huntington Foresters volleyball team who has dealt with some fairly traumatic things over the last year and a half. She's still dealing with them, in fact.

On Aug. 26, 2016, her first day of college, Eakright was diagnosed as having an extremely rare form of cancer that usually affects children in their first five years of life. Instead of going through freshman orientation, she and her parents were describing her diagnosis during a team meeting. Despite undergoing a couple of surgeries and getting chemotherapy treatments, she played through the season, earning freshman all-league honors, before undergoing a year of treatments that she hated. Even today, she can't visit the hospital without throwing up first because she associates the place with chemotherapy, sickness and vomit.

Yeah, normal could be pretty good.

"I think the new normal is just going to be better than the old normal was in every aspect of my life," she said. "It changed my perspective on everything I do and everyone I'm around and volleyball and school. It's just going to be better than it was before, and I'm thankful for that. I'm not thankful that it happened, but I'm thankful for the outcome that I have and the people I met and everything that happened with it."

Eakright had to miss last volleyball season, sitting on the bench as a volunteer assistant coach and trying to help in any way she could with encouragement or tips. The important part was being around her teammates, who had been so supportive. Huntington coach Kyle Shondell said Eakright was the team member who had the most impact on the season even though she never played.

Still, she had no idea it would hurt so much, because she

wanted to play so badly.

"She called crying during the first match and saying it was so hard," said her father, Craig, a pastor at Grace Gathering in New Haven.

Eakright desperately wanted to be out on the court helping her teammates, who were helping her survive. She was still wearing a chemotherapy port in her chest, and neuropathy meant she couldn't bend her feet properly or jump, but really that was the least of what she went through.

Because the first three chemotherapy treatments were so strong, they almost killed her, and a fourth was canceled. After each treatment, she couldn't eat for days. That was just the first three. After surgery, there were 26 more treatments to go. In all, she had 46 days of chemotherapy, and more than half of those days included multiple doses of two or three different types. She tried to fight through it all on her own.

"Most people didn't know because she kind of hid it," said her mother, Jill. "From the very beginning, she never wanted anybody to feel sorry for her. Most of the time, people didn't realize how hard it really was on her, especially after the surgery was done and she had 26 weeks more chemo to go."

There was always a balance of how much to keep private and what to share with others. What's the best way to handle it — with privacy so there's the focus to fight, or publicly so there's plenty of help?

"From the very beginning, we've been like, the more people who know, the more who can pray," Craig Eakright said.

Except at first, Paige wasn't so sure if she wanted anyone to know. That wasn't selfishness, but actually, empathy.

"I'm definitely one of those people who hate when people are upset, and I didn't want them to be sad for me," she said. "I wanted to make friends at school because I'm normal, not because I'm abnormal. They reacted just the way I wanted them to. I asked all my best friends to treat me the same, and they treated me like I was a normal person, but they comforted me when I needed comforting. The way everyone reacted was exactly what I needed."

Whenever she came home from a treatment, neighbors would decorate the Eakright front door. Anonymous letters and food were dropped off, and trips to her surgeon in Detroit were paid for. Everyone stepped up.

"There's a lot of blessings through what she's gone through, and you're like, 'I hope we did it right,'" her mother said. "So many people we need to thank, and 'Thank you' is just such a small two-word saying that never seems to be enough. It just doesn't give enough, but there are so many we are grateful for."

And then there was the family's faith. They continually repeated Romans 8:28, which says, "And we know that in all things God works for the good of those who love him, who have been called according to his purpose." They may not have known the reason for this challenge, but they know one will be revealed eventually.

"From the very beginning, we knew this doesn't feel like it, but it's for our good and for His glory," Craig said. "Those are the two things we held onto even during the painful part of it. It had to be something big He has plans for."

Maybe it was simply to inspire others with the way Paige handled the situation. Sure, as anyone would, she cried and had a breakdown about once a week, but even then, she learned from the experiences.

"I wouldn't cry around people, so I would have meltdowns by myself," she said. "Usually, I kept it to myself until I realized that my friends were going to be there for me and it didn't matter."

But without realizing it, she became an inspiration to the rest of her Empowered Volleyball Club members. She kept showing up to help out, train and just be around.

"As we began to come around Paige and her family, she never seemed rattled by the enormous fight in front of her," said Empowered Volleyball Club co-owner Ashley Robbins. "What a powerful example to put entire faith in our creator Jesus Christ. ... How on earth could anyone complain about how hard (training) was when Paige was doing the same workout with her chemo port visible?"

Maybe the most reinforcing sign during those first months after surgery was that it seemed every time she turned on the radio, Chris Tomlin was singing "Good Good Father." There were a ton of those kinds of emotional moments that reminded her how God was with her and that it was going to be OK.

And maybe soon. She started workouts last week and hopes to play some this spring in preparation for next fall's schedule. It's going to take time, and she has to be patient with her body. Now she needs even more encouragement from her teammates, who have supported her so much.

"The main thing is to figure out how to jump again, because

that's going to be the hardest thing for me," Paige said. "My team is really good about supporting me when I'm playing. It may never be 100 percent how it was, but I think in the volleyball aspect of it, I can only get better, and I'll be better than I was before, and in faith, I'll be better than I was before."

She has survived, outlasted cancer. But her body is only 50 percent back, well behind her outlook and optimism.

"If anybody has the ability to play volleyball without the feeling in your feet, it's Paige Eakright, because she's done far more impressive things than that," Shondell said. "She may have had doubts through the entire process, but we never did. We knew she was going to beat this because she's a fighter and that's who she is. She was too stubborn for cancer."

Eakright is studying to be a teacher and wonders if maybe God's point of all this is to help some student in the future deal with something similar. Maybe it was just to inspire others, which she's already pretty good at.

"When I spoke at the school, the pastor asked me what I wanted to take away from all this," she said. "The only thing I had was just for college students not to take anything for granted, because I definitely did before all this. Literally, everything — eating, walking, sleeping, family — I took all of that for granted at least a little bit, and I don't at all anymore. I can't imagine not having any of those things."

"I told the athletes, 'If you are playing your sport and complaining about it, stop. I literally can't play the one thing I love more than anything. Nothing in this life is worth taking for granted.'"

Yeah, a little normal might be what she needs the most.

CHAPTER 3
Volleyball coaches' love story is based on redemption
Published Sept. 13, 2016, in The News-Sentinel

Partly because she was a star high school and college athlete, Ashlee Robbins desperately wants to beat her husband, Will, in an athletic event. She once came as close as clearing the solids in a pool game before scratching on the eight ball. Though Will constantly reminds her of it, he has yet to play her again.

So last month, when Ashlee's Leo girls volleyball team beat Will's Lakewood Park Christian team in the West Noble Invitational championship match, he still had the guts to say, "You will still never beat me in anything athletic."

Will is either incredibly brave or very stupid. Has any husband ever really won a trash-talking battle with his wife? Or are the few who have just too smart to remember or mention it publicly?

This Saturday, there's another chance for a rare husband-versus-wife high school coaching confrontation, but the Lions and the Panthers need to win their respective pools to meet in the Leo Invitational championship match. That prospect might cause trouble in some marriages, but the Robbinses figure it's another chance for some laughs and for their very good teams to keep improving.

"Even though we're super-competitive, when it comes down to the teams we coach, we have a relationship where we enjoy working together and supporting each other," Will said. "I would love to see her go to state in (Class) 3A and us in 1A. If we were both in 3A, then it would be ugly because we are so competitive, but this has actually worked out phenomenally well."

They are excellent coaches and partners in the Empowered Sports Club, they are still extremely successful players and Ashlee is the math department chair at Leo. They also are deeply faithful Christians who have a strong calling for serving youth, and those things give their marriage a strong base, which is amazing because theirs is a love story no one could have predicted.

Though both played volleyball at IPFW, they never met on campus, because Will, 39, is seven years older than Ashlee, and as she was graduating from Leo in 2002, he was starting a seven-year stint in federal prison. He played at IPFW from 1995 to 1997, including sitting out a year for poor grades, and then was going to transfer in 1998. Though plenty of people tried to help him, he got into trouble instead and was eventually convicted of bank robbery.

"Up until that point, I also had six state cases," he said. "I got into selling drugs and partying and doing things to maintain that lifestyle. I had to experience it myself, because I was wild enough and hard-headed enough that nobody could tell me anything. I just had to experience it for myself and fail on my own, which I did terribly."

He used his time in prison to reform, rehabilitate a knee injury and finish his degree. He also became a believer.

"Prison was the best thing for me," he said. "It took me out of society, and there were strict enough consequences that it opened my eyes and made me ask what I was doing with my life. It set me apart for a period of time where I could study, work out, rehab, get back in shape, and get a solid foundation in the Word and try to figure out who I was in Christ and what my purpose was."

When he was released at Christmas 2008, Ashlee was early in her teaching career at Leo. Seeing how he had turned his life around, the IPFW volleyball alumni enveloped him and invited him to play at the Doble Classic in Dearborn, Mich., which draws adult teams from all over the Midwest. There, he found some food and sat in the stands to watch his sister Angie's team play.

"He is actually sitting in the stands eating our food," said Ashlee, who was a teammate of Angie Robbins but didn't realize the connection. "We yelled at him, 'Stop eating our food!' We ended up winning the tournament, but they didn't, so they had to leave early."

The next day, she received a note from former IPFW player Jorge Ralat asking her to play in the Saint Francis Invitational the next weekend. Turns out, Will also was on that team.

"We won the tournament, we went out for ice cream, and actually I met his mom, and the rest is history," Ashlee said.

The next weekend, Will and Ashlee drove to Kokomo to hear a pastor and author speak. They were inseparable after that, dating for three months before getting engaged. She was everything he had been praying for, but her parents, the Roths, made them wait a year to get married, because like a lot of people, they had questions. Everyone was looking out for her and wondering if she knew what Will was all about.

"I didn't believe that he had done those things, because that was not the person I knew, so it wasn't hard for me," Ashlee said. "I didn't see that person even though everybody told me about him. He was not that person, though that was a hard step to get people to accept. When he told my dad about his story, my dad said, 'If you have truly changed, the only person that can change you is God.'"

"I have to give her credit," Will said. He agrees that it was only because the Roths are such a strong Christian family who believed in God's power that they allowed him a chance to prove his redemption.

Will and Ashlee were married in 2010, and he now speaks frequently to youngsters about his story. They are two of the area's better volleyball coaches, and their teams are all in on the "rivalry," too.

"I hope that he wins his pool (this weekend), because it was a fun experience the first time," Ashlee said with a wicked grin.

"Let me beat her just one time," he said, folding his hands as if in prayer.

She knows exactly how he feels.

CHAPTER 4
Katie Graham is taking the fight to her abusive past
Published Dec. 13, 2017, on News-Sentinel.com

When Melissa Connor was a first-year head coach and Katie Graham was a freshman player in the Heritage High School girls basketball program, they were waiting for rides after a game one night. The coach asked if the player's father ever came to watch her play.

"She shared that she doesn't see her dad and he had abused her when she was little," Connor recalled. "'It's OK, my mom adopted me when I was little. ... I've dealt with this for 12 years.'"

Connor cried the whole ride home and, two years later, still tears up at the memory.

What's the deepest secret you've ever shared with a friend, something otherwise you'd bury so deep inside not even Lara Croft could have a hope of finding it? Would you dare? Or would you just hold it all inside and hope that somehow, someday, it would just go away and that if you ignored it long enough, you'd never have to deal with it?

You'd hide it, wouldn't you? Almost everyone would.

NOT YOUR AVERAGE TEENAGER

But Katie Graham is unique, especially among teenagers. She's shared her secret with her friends, and now she wants to share it with others. It's horrible, life-altering, but she's not letting what happened when she was 4 have any power over her or her choices. It won't define her, and she's sure as hell done letting it hinder her. She'll define her own life, thank you.

She was the wrong kid to pick a fight with. Now she'll lean in for more, daring her past to try and take another swing at her. Bring it on, because she's ready to swing a leg right back where it hurts.

Because her birth parents had some pretty severe issues, Katie went into foster care when she was 13 months old. After a year and a half and during a stay in her second foster home, Graham was adopted by Scott Graham and his wife, Tracey. She finally had a stable future.

Then one day, her mother drove home from attending a friend's out-of-town funeral to find Katie coming down the stairs saying something had happened with her father that she had no comprehension was illegal and immoral.

"She just told me like it was nothing," said Tracey, Katie's mother, who now has the last name of Piering. "I looked at him, and he said, 'We need to talk.' I got the kids upstairs playing, and when I went downstairs, I was just sobbing. I just didn't know what to do at that point. Shortly after that, I got them all put into bed and I called the police, and at 3 a.m., they came and got him."

Scott Graham was sentenced to 15 years in prison after he admitted molesting his daughter five to 10 times over a year-long period.

"There was an instance probably a month before where she said something very strange, and not something I thought was OK," Piering said. "I went and talked to him about it, but he explained it away. It made me feel terrible. I felt like something was happening because she had a lot of signs, but I felt like it had to have been happening in foster care because she was always with me or her dad."

After moving the family in with her parents, Piering started her three children in counseling and filed for divorce. She rebuilt her life by focusing almost completely on her children, fighting her own feelings of guilt, too.

DEALING WITH THE AFTERMATH

More than 10 years later, Graham is a junior at Heritage, where she runs cross country and track and loves basketball. She's usually Connor's first player off the bench, providing the Patriots with some energy, some aggression or a competitive boost. No matter the score, she never quits.

It's a trait she's earned every day of her life. Instead of being timid or tentative because of the things that happened, she chooses to be proactive. She's told some of her friends, and she realizes everyone else will know when this story is published. To her, it would be worse to keep something like this a secret, trying to hide it and ignore it. That's why destructive acts such as this have such intimidating power.

These actions need to be exposed, confronted and attacked, she believes.

"I'm pretty open about it usually," Graham said. "I don't know how to describe it, but I feel like I've benefited more from it. If this can help someone else, yeah, it needs to be out there."

LOOKING AHEAD

Choosing to look at the circumstances as something to build off of was a decision Graham made, a brutally difficult, gut-wrenching process she has fought to the other side of where she doesn't have any regrets. It happened, but not to the person she is now. That would be giving in, and the fire in her eyes shows she never will.

"To have someone go through trauma at a young age, and then have repeat trauma, she's a very big success story," Connor said. "Then on top of it, her attitude and perseverance and mental strength about everything, I preach that daily in the gym, and she is definitely one of my mentally tough girls.

I cannot ask for anything more."

Well, she could and probably will, and Graham will respond.

But Graham doesn't see herself as anything special, just a person who dealt with what was in front of her because she had to. It's not there anymore because she has passed it by. She understands how others like her mother and coach can see her as exceptional because of her excellent grades, her attitude, her work ethic and her compassion, but she's a little embarrassed to hear the compliments. Those are about things she has done, not necessarily what she wants to do. Those things will allow her to become who she wants to be.

Overcoming and taking credit for it means admitting that what happened affected her negatively, means saying the effects might be permanent. She won't accept that. Sure, Father's Day and the holidays sometimes can be troubling, but they aren't tougher than she is.

"If something is happening, even if things have been (tough)," she said. "I was fortunate to have my mom. There are so many girls, maybe even in my school, who things like this might be happening to, and they don't tell anyone because they are scared of what might happen. If you don't tell anyone and just keep it inside, it will just keep coming faster and faster, and you won't be able to do great things because it will always be a part of you."

She is different, though, and some of the things she says and believes sound more like a woman aged 26 than 16. After Heritage and after college, she wants to serve in the Peace Corps and then teach troubled kids, a goal she told her mother when she was in the third or fourth grade, even before she started playing basketball. Asked what she might be doing in 10 years, Graham immediately says working in another country helping people, doing whatever God wants her to do.

"She's a very good example of, 'Life happens, and this is how you respond to it,'" Connor said. "One of the things about Katie that I see is she doesn't think she's different. She doesn't feel like she has this advantage on other people. Because she has been through it, she is so compassionate to other people. She doesn't feel like she has to conform to anything right now. If she doesn't want to do it, she's not going to. In this generation specifically, you don't see that a lot, especially in teenage girls. That's not Katie. She goes out and does her thing and does the best she can for her teammates and her family, and that's just what she's going to do."

WHY TELL ANYONE NOW?

Graham thinks she can help others who may be facing what she endured. She's unwilling to wait until she's older when she can do something positive now, which is why she's telling her story.

"I just want to help someone if I can," she said, chin up, eyes forward and with a determined voice. "Lots of people ignore facts these days. They try to push it to the side. There are so many people who are bullies to one another, and they have no idea what the other person is going through."

She won't stand for that, which is why she told her friends, because they needed to know. She hates anything fake among her circle, she said, and not telling them would have been fake, dishonest with those you are supposed to be the most honest with.

Yes, all this happened to Katie Graham, and she's never understood why, but its power over her is done. Maybe, she believes, God gave this to her because she could handle it and make something positive out of it to help others. She will discover the purpose and fulfill it.

"There's still a lot of stuff I have to figure out," she said. "Life hits you sometimes, and you just can't dwell on it."

Her future is too bright for that, and there are too many things to accomplish to allow her past to determine her future. She's going to do that herself.

Her mother always told Graham she wasn't a victim, she was a survivor. She's really a conqueror.

CHAPTER 5
Jack Prindle traveled a long, hard path to peace
Published Feb. 1, 2005, in The News-Sentinel

The other day, Komets defenseman Troy Neumeier said he wished he could be as laid-back as Jack Prindle. It seems no matter what happens, the hockey team's assistant equipment manager just glides through life. But that's because he's seen and done much, much more than your average 56-year-old.

"I tell the guys that I think everybody should go through a

traumatic experience once in their life, only because it makes you appreciate what you have," Prindle said. "I think you become a better person. You look at people a lot different."

Besides his calm demeanor, Prindle is also known for being able to recall exactly the defining moments in his life, although there are many he'd like to forget.

After growing up on the corner of Dewald and Broadway streets in Fort Wayne, Ind., and attending Central High School, Prindle was fed up with the strict lifestyle of his parents, so he chose another one, enlisting in the Marine Corps at age 17. Instead of the shirt and tie his parents required him to wear, he put on a new uniform two months after he turned 18.

"I thought I wanted something more exciting," he said.

He went through boot camp in San Diego and then was sent to Camp Pendleton. In June 1968, he entered the Vietnam War at Da Nang. He arrived a couple of months after the Viet Cong's Tet Offensive. Prindle won't be specific about what he saw or did in Vietnam, except to say that he was a sniper and sometimes spent as much as a month at a time living in trees. There was no one else to talk to for weeks, and any movement or noise meant possible discovery — and death.

"After a while, you didn't know what you were there for," he said. "You could say you were helping people, or you thought you were at times. Little kids in the daytime would be your friends, and at night, they'd turn on you in a heartbeat."

He took part in two tours and five operations, and says the movie "Full Metal Jacket" is as close as Hollywood has come to what the tension was really like. The stress finally built to where he couldn't function, and nightmares forced him out of the military. He was ruled unfit for military duty and given a general discharge under honorable conditions.

That was only the start of his hard road through life.

After being discharged in April 1970, Prindle was given medication and sent home to Fort Wayne, where he married the first girl he ever dated. Her brother got him a job at International Harvester, and soon a son and a daughter were born. That was the positive side of life.

"I was drinking really, really heavy, and my wife wanted to get me some help," Prindle said. "I said I didn't have a drinking problem, but I was acting weird, such as sleeping in my car and not coming home, and I started missing work. The only way they would let me back was if I saw a psychiatrist."

A doctor recommended Prindle be admitted to Parkview South Unit where shock treatments were ordered to help eliminate the nightmares. First thing in the morning, nurses would grease up his
ankles, wrists, temples and sides and give him a shot to put him to sleep. A rubber bit was put in his mouth so he wouldn't swallow his tongue.

"When they put the shot in your arm, it felt like your head would explode," he said. "You'd wake up and never know where you were for a while. You felt like a zombie.

"At the time, if I smelled something or something caught my eye, (my) mind would race right back there. (The treatment) did work pretty well."

The treatments were held Monday, Wednesday and Friday mornings until 20 were completed. After eight months, Prindle was released to return to his marriage and his job, but unfortunately, to his drinking as well.

"I put my wife through a lot. I'd show up and I'd leave again. I had no business being married. I wasn't fit to live with."

His wife eventually got a restraining order, but after she would leave for work in the morning, Prindle would crawl in through a window and sleep off his drinking. They finally divorced in 1980. Three times, Prindle tried to re-enlist with the Marine Corps, the last time at age 35.

"There was something about it I just missed," he said. "Maybe it was the thrill. You come back here and get married, which was fine, but that wears off and your mind is always somewhere else."

He was living off insurance checks from Harvester and had plenty of drinking buddies who would support his habit when he didn't have the money. Eventually, however, he became homeless. For two years, he often lived under bridges. He eventually checked himself back into Parkview for 10 more rounds of shock treatments in early 1979. There, he met a woman, and they moved in together that November using money the Veterans Administration paid him. He also got his job back at Harvester — but the drinking continued.

"I thought I was a big shot, bringing home steaks, and of course bringing home beer, too. May 25, 1980, I had one of my drinking binges, scared her and she took off."

He was crushed, falling into a fog of alcohol, doubt and self-pity, and didn't pay his rent for months. The sheriff's department evicted him, and Prindle returned to the streets. For a while, he lived out of a 1963 Chevy, until he sold it for $30 or $40, which he spent drinking. Often he'd eat at St. Mary's Soup Kitchen or at the Rescue Mission. He hitchhiked to Florida twice.

"Don't go through Ohio, because it's a booger to get picked up there," he said. "Down in Kentucky and Tennessee, all they wanted to do was party, and that's all I wanted to do."

He recalls going to Komets games, picking up enough aluminum cans to buy cigarettes, a ticket and a bottle of rum. Then he'd pour the rum into a soda at the coliseum. One night, he passed out in Section 31, woke up at 1 a.m. and tried walking home to the bridge, but passed out again. The grass was long, he said, but that's about all he remembers.

He was trying to figure things out, he said, and having a pity party. There was no direction in his life, and he wasn't sure if he really wanted to find one.

"I remember when I was in my heyday drinking, I'd look in the mirror and see my bloodshot eyes and curse myself out," he said. "'You worthless bastard.' I'd stay off the booze for a day and then go right back into it."

In June 1983, a buddy suggested they take a bus to Las Vegas and live in the desert. The only problem was the buddy got scared and left for home the day after they arrived — but didn't tell Prindle. After a while, he couldn't get into the casinos anymore, so he would clip coupons for free hot dogs and Cokes to survive.

He stayed on the streets of Las Vegas for a month, then

checked into a Salvation Army Clinic for a year of alcohol rehabilitation. He also found religion while watching a Billy Graham Crusade on television. Somehow, he felt the message was directed at him.

"I came to the end of the road," he said. "I had nowhere else to go. Anything else there is in life, I tried it, and none of it worked. It always left you empty because it's not meant to fulfill you."

He came out of rehab and returned to the Las Vegas streets. A buddy and some of his friends took a vacation to Las Vegas in 1984 and saved enough money for Prindle to get a bus ride home. He stayed with some friends for more than a year, trying to get his life together.

"I finally started to taper off from the booze," he said. "I could see myself going back in the same position again, and I think I just got sick of it. Maybe I looked at the past and said, "This isn't worth it.' I realized I had not only made a mess of my life but a lot of people's."

After coming home, he found summer employment with Galbreath Landscaping. He received unemployment during the winters but one day in 1989 decided he needed something to do, so he went to McMillen Park Ice Arena to learn to skate. He was 40 years old and started playing pickup hockey as a goaltender.

Then in 1993, on the last day of pickup hockey for the year, he was leaving the arena when manager Mitzi Toepfer asked if he'd like a job. He'd be responsible for cleaning the building late at night and making sure the ice was ready to go the next day.

That fall, he stuck around after his overnight shift and set up some of the Komets players' equipment, organizing sticks and filling water bottles to help equipment manager Joe Franke, who has become Prindle's mentor. Eventually, Prindle started to work full time for the team during the season and for the Parks and Recreation Department during the summers. Now, he practically lives at the rink, often arriving before 6 a.m. When he's not there, he's usually doing something with his son or daughter and his three grandsons and three granddaughters. He repaired his relationship with his kids in 1986 and said they never held anything against him.

"They've never said one negative thing," he said.

So, no, very little flusters Jack Prindle these days.

"I took a hard road to get here, but I think it's the only road I had," he said. "Maybe I used that stuff as an excuse to do what I wanted to do. You have to remember it was my choice to live on the streets. I wanted that lifestyle because it made me think back. I used to be bitter, but I'm not anymore."

He loves being around the Komets, finally finding the camaraderie he had searched for since leaving the Marine Corps. Now he looks forward to the next day and sleeps only about four hours a night. The players and former players know that and often call in the middle of the night to talk. After a life spent trying to miss everything, now he doesn't want to miss anything.

"You know what I told these guys? I love getting older. It's more fun. Right now, I wouldn't trade what I went through. Look where I'm at now: I'm the happiest I've ever been. I see the Lord leading me, and I know I'm on the path I'm supposed to be."

In a life scarred by war and his own personal battles, Prindle has finally found peace.

CHAPTER 6
Longtime area tennis teacher has new goals and dreams
Published Jan. 27, 2016, on News-Sentinel.com

One day last fall, a young teenage boy was riding his bike up to a stoplight at an intersection in central Fort Wayne, Ind. He looked over to see a man, who was wearing a plastic blue football helmet without the face mask, walking toward him.

"Hey, how are you?" the man asked. "Hey, do you know why I'm wearing a blue helmet? I was in a bicycle accident. You are too good-looking a kid to have this happen to you, so would you do me a favor? Christmas is coming up, and if you don't have a helmet, maybe ask for one for Christmas so you don't have to go through this situation. Could you do that for me? I don't want this to ever happen to anybody else."

Then the light changed, and the boy rode off while the man in the helmet slowly resumed his journey.

* * *

Of course, originally, there was a girl involved. Don Offerle was a Bishop Dwenger High School student who wanted to stay close to a girl over the summer, so he applied to be a lifeguard at Pine Valley Country Club where she hung out. There was no opening, but the Fort Wayne Parks and Recreation Department had one and hired him. The department needed somebody to vacuum the pool at 7 a.m., so he said he'd do it. The department also needed somebody to run the recreation leagues at Swinney Park, so he did that, too.

He became known as the guy who would volunteer for everything and get the job done well. He'd work from 7 a.m. until 11 p.m. and sometimes invite friends to play tennis until midnight. He wasn't any good, usually getting smoked, but he had fun. Desperate to improve, he asked for advice from teaching pro Tim Sullivan, who suggested books by Vic Braden.

When someone came by asking for a lesson, Offerle figured he'd try, using the principles from the books. The player was impressed and suggested Offerle to others.

After graduating from Bishop Dwenger in 1981, Offerle read a story in local college IPFW's student newspaper about the new tennis team looking for players. Sullivan happened to be the coach. Despite all his passion, Offerle wasn't very good, serving most often as an extra. In fact, he never played until one night when the opponent showed up with an extra player. When Offerle asked for advice, Sullivan simply said, "Don't get hurt."

Offerle worked hard and eventually improved enough to play No. 2 singles for IPFW. Then he coached at Fort Wayne Country Club for a year before becoming the coach at Harding High School for seven years and at New Haven High School for four more. Like his own path, he'd take hopeless situations and help players improve more than they dreamed, and somehow win a few matches as a team.

While keeping up the private lessons, Offerle became the original pro at Autumn Ridge Golf Club and then at Cherry Hill Golf Club. He didn't use traditional instruction, but he was successful. His love of the sport was more than infectious;

it was addictive. He could make people believe they could improve — and they would.

That's how he fell in love with tennis. The girl married somebody else.

* * *

For fun and because he worked with children and liked to stay fit, Offerle would ride his bike all over the county and sometimes beyond if the wind was pushing the right direction. He acquired a 12-speed Miyata but was always extra careful on it, scared by newspaper articles about people dying in bike accidents. He always rode assuming a car couldn't see him.

After riding more than 4,000 miles over the previous summers, he rode the Hilly Hundred race through southern Indiana in 2014, purchasing a helmet in a thrift shop to follow the rules. He lost it afterward, never thinking that riding was a life-threatening situation since he had never known anyone who had been in a serious accident.

Last May, the Offerle family was preparing to leave for a Florida vacation. Offerle was going to stay at his brother Tom's house, so he rode his bike through the IPFW campus, over a bridge and onto California Road behind the Red Cross. It was about 11 p.m., but there were no cars out, and he was continuing to be very careful as he crossed Parnell Avenue.

* * *

No one knows what really happened that night, especially Offerle. Police don't think he was hit by a car, but maybe he rode over an unseen pothole or possibly a speed bump, flipped over his bike and landed on his unprotected head. No one knows how long he lay in the shopping center's parking lot.

Eventually, maybe just in time, someone discovered him, but no one knows who; the call was anonymous. As Offerle was rushed to Parkview Regional Medical Center, police found his cell phone and called the last number used to notify a family member. When his nephews arrived, they were told he might not survive the night.

Dr. James Dozier, a neurosurgeon, saved Offerle's life by persuading the family to let him remove a hand-size piece of Offerle's skull on the left side to relieve brain swelling. Days later, family members were told he might not get any better. Somehow he kept hanging on.

For a month, Offerle stayed at the medical center, but he doesn't remember any of it. Even when coherent, he didn't recognize some family members.

Then he spent a month at Parkview Hospital on Randallia Drive, continuing to heal as family members were encouraged to find a nursing home. When Offerle finally regained full consciousness, he asked his brother Tom why he was in the hospital.

At the request of family members, Offerle spent 40 days at Hope Network Neuro Rehabilitation Center in Coldwater, Mich. He could walk around but was required to wear a blue helmet, and on Nov. 12, the missing part of his skull was replaced.

* * *

Friends kept praying, even gathering on the courts at Autumn Ridge where a "Pray for Donny O" sign was arranged on the fence. Denise Brower started a Facebook page, "Donny O, he's my pro ... fan and prayer club," which attracted more than 400 members. A rumor started that Offerle had died, so he posted a video July 5 thanking everyone for their love and prayers.

How do people ever know how blessed they are until they come up against something and everybody they know steps up?

"It's only because of those prayers that I'm still here," Offerle said. "Prayer definitely works. I was a very good believer before all this happened. I even talked about God and even got yelled at once for bringing up Christ during a lesson. My faith after this accident has totally increased. The Lord was my savior before, and now he's my best friend."

Offerle has always been the guy who does things for everyone else, the guy everybody owes favors because he never reclaims them. With his injuries, he's had to learn to surrender his life to someone else.

But somehow he has survived and continues to recover. He's committed to teaching tennis again, and he swears he'll definitely ride again, this time with a helmet.

He spends his time thanking friends and family and, whenever he can, talking about the need to wear a helmet. As his sister said, he has learned to drink in life's blessings, and he has become a modern-day prophet enthused by a new message.

"My mission is to get the word out, and I am totally convinced that's why I'm here," he said. "I want my tragedy and what happened to help others. It's something I don't want anyone else to have to go through."

* * *

Recently, a woman stepped into the South Bend, Ind., office of

John Offerle, an optometrist, saying, "You're about to see my 13-year-old son in your next appointment, and he's a biker just like your brother, but he will not wear a helmet. Could you do me a favor and talk to him?"

So John Offerle sat the boy down and told him about his brother, who was so injured from a bicycle accident that he didn't recognize his older brother. The doctor wasn't sure how much the boy had listened but hoped somehow his message got through.

About 10 days later, a letter arrived in the office.

"Dr. John Offerle, I want to thank you for saving my son's life," it began. "He was involved in a bicycle accident and cracked the helmet in half. He suffered a broken eye socket, and that's all."

CHAPTER 7
Broadcaster didn't give up when turned down
Published July 18, 2015, in The News-Sentinel

Though he has a face made for newspapers and the speaking voice of a high school geometry teacher, somehow Mike Maahs is celebrating his 25th year in local sports broadcasting. His story revolves around having faith in himself and the nerve to introduce himself to famous broadcasters and ask for advice.

And then having a ton of God-given patience.

Though Maahs, 62, doesn't have a broadcaster's shtick, he has called almost 1,200 Fort Wayne Wizards/TinCaps games and more than 800 IPFW athletic events by just being himself. He calls what he sees using his natural personality, passion and enthusiasm, and those are enough to bring the listener into the scene. Those things, and the love of his wife, Sue, have sustained him when anyone else would have given up to take a "real" job.

Oh, yes, mostly because of broadcasting, he's also had only part-time jobs since coming to Fort Wayne, Ind., in 1987.

"There have been times when she's wanted me to jump in a lake and get a real job, but I can't do it," he said. "She has always supported me."

Even when it meant he had to work in mall security, selling cell phones, overnight hotel desk jobs, local golf shops and now the IPFW fitness center. In addition to Fort Wayne baseball and IPFW sports, his media resume includes almost everything Fort Wayne has to offer: high school basketball and football, University of Saint Francis football, Tri-State University athletics, Fury basketball, radio shows and coaches' TV shows, along with writing for both The News-Sentinel and Journal Gazette newspapers.

Maahs' greatest ability is to get back up after he's been fired, lied to repeatedly, ignored, taken for granted or overlooked for the better-looking, smoother and more polished competition. Mostly, that's what happens until someone says, "Hey, we need a broadcaster immediately," and Maahs happens to be standing right there.

Now he's found a home by being the most giving, loyal, humble, honest and respected announcer in the Midwest League, the only guy to call the last 11 All-Star Games. Everybody owes him at least one favor because he never calls his in.

"Part of it is if I can help somebody out, somebody will help me out sometime down the road," he said.

His only true failing is that his postgame shows last longer than presidential news conferences because he doesn't like to give up the microphone. No one is better at replaying a 2-1 game in 45 minutes. Sometimes TinCaps President Mike Nutter waits until he has driven home to call after games because he knows Maahs will still be on the air.

"He is so passionate and so loyal," Nutter said. "He's a guy I love, and I can use that word with all sincerity. You could run him into a wall, and he'd ask what was next. I can count on one hand the number of times I've heard him complain about anything. The only time he's hard on something is himself. Go golfing with him sometime and listen to him talk to himself. It's hilarious!"

Maahs' life story is more unrelenting than a late-inning rally. While growing up in Detroit and Bay City, Mich., he thought he wanted to be a history teacher and coach, a minister or a broadcaster and/or sportswriter. He's done all those things since he came to Fort Wayne in 1987 to attend the Concordia Lutheran Seminary.

Early-morning Greek lessons and trying to support a family stopped that, but one day, he and Sue were in a bookstore when Maahs recognized a WLAB radio personality's voice, so he introduced himself. A few weeks later, station general manager Jim Zix called to ask whether Maahs would be interested in calling local high school sports, something Maahs had trained himself to do by talking into a tape recorder while sitting in the stands at games.

On Jan. 3, 1990, Maahs and Zix had set up the equipment

before the reserve game at Concordia Lutheran High School when Zix said he'd buy Maahs dinner. That's when a startled Maahs was informed he'd be the play-by-play guy. His color analyst that night? Jim Zix. It all worked out because Matt Dellinger hit a half-court shot at the buzzer to beat South Side, and Maahs had a new calling. That's when his rotisserie of part-time broadcasting jobs really started.

Three times, Maahs applied to be the Wizards' radio announcer and was turned down. In 2002, he became an official scorer and started a friendship with broadcaster Terry Byrum, calling 36 games in 2003 and 2004. When Byrum left in 2005, Maahs once again applied for the primary announcer's spot, and this time it was his for good.

"It's hard to imagine any partner who could be easier to work with coming into a new situation, and that's just Mike's personality," said TinCaps broadcaster John Nolan, who came to Fort Wayne in 2013. "Right from that first lunch, I felt comfortable with him."

Maahs loves broadcasting and knows in his heart it's what God wants him to do. Ask him why, and each sentence starts with "Fortunately," or "I've been fortunate."

"I think it's because I love what I do," he said. "Every year on my last broadcast, I say it's an honor and a privilege to do this. I don't know why, but I love what I do. You know you've done your job when a listener reaches out and tells you they feel like they are right there because of what you do."

But after calling 2,000 games, does he ever feel he can relax and enjoy his successful career?

"I keep trying to work at that," he said. "There are a few times when I let my guard down, but part of it is my upbringing. My parents always taught me to treat people the way you want to be treated and don't let your head get too high in the air."

No one should tell him, but after 25 years, he's already part of the fabric of the community.

CHAPTER 8
Lifter finds uplifting strength from faith
Published June 29, 2017, on News-Sentinel.com

"Whatever you do, work at it with all your heart, as working for the Lord, not for human masters."
Colossians 3:23

What Danielle Douglas, 25, calls her lifting verse is proudly printed down her warm-up's right arm. The powerlifter is hoping fellow competitors or anyone else will ask what it means, because she loves to tell them.

"For me, my strength is a way to reach out to people," she said. "Some people can sing really well, talk really well or cook really well, and that's how they serve people, but my strength gives me that opportunity."

That makes sense, and she makes it sound easy, but it took Douglas a few different tries to find her calling, with God jerking the leash a couple of times to get her back on the path he had for her. Like anyone else, she had to try her own way a few times before eventually giving in and submitting to her true mission.

Now she holds four state records, ranks 28th nationally in her weight class and is building an unbelievable future with so many possibilities for competition and witnessing.

"I keep my eyes always on the Lord. With him at my right hand, I will not be shaken."
Psalm 16:8

When Douglas was a senior at Carroll High School, she took a weightlifting class taught by Jeremy Hartman.

She had tried volleyball and soccer, but lifting seemed to drag her in more and more.

"I played around with it, and I was good at it for some reason," she said. "There's always a challenge, and you are always moving forward to reach goals, and then you set newer and crazier goals. The other sports, I was mediocre at, and I don't like to be mediocre."

She's always been a bit of a perfectionist who found motivation when told she probably couldn't do something. A little bit of bullheadedness can go a long way in an individual sport sometimes. Douglas maxed out as a senior with 135 pounds on the bench, 225 squatting and 250 on the deadlift.

But she wasn't satisfied. Though she found her professional niche at IPFW with an associate's degree in dental laboratory technology, she kept trying new things in the gym to fill her competitive need.

"For I know the plans I have for you," declares the Lord, "plans to prosper you and not to harm you, plans to give you hope and a future."
Jeremiah 29:11

At first, Douglas was attracted to bodybuilding because, in part, she wanted the attention the sport brought. She improved, but at 5 feet 2 inches, her ability needed a few more inches in height to go very far. It also didn't fit her modest nature, and she found herself staying away from people socially because her training didn't allow her to eat what they were eating.

So she tried mixed martial arts. In three fights, she was 1-2, and her mother cried from watching.

"It was one of those things that really sounded cool at the time," she said. "I just wanted to show people I was tough. I don't think I had my priorities in necessarily the right places."

Posing in a sports bra or punching someone else in the face didn't fit with her personal beliefs too well, either, so there was always an internal struggle to justify it. In the end, she simply couldn't believe this was God's plan.

"She is clothed with strength and dignity; she can laugh at the days to come."
Proverbs 31:25

"When I was doing those things, I think I was looking to find fulfillment, but I would never find it," Douglas said. "That's where social media comes in. When you are female and you post something about fighting, you are going to get attention. I think I wanted that attention and fulfillment with every 'Like.' It was not until I realized that I was never going to get that fulfillment through social media, that it had to come from above, and the only way I was going to get it was by looking up."

She needed to find something that was glorifying to God, and the bodybuilding and the fighting weren't very humble or meek, either. It just didn't fit with how she was raised, or who she felt she was supposed to be. She didn't feel the acceptance in her heart.

"I always had my hands clenched or in my pockets, and it wasn't until I opened my hands and said, 'I'm yours,' (that it felt right)," she said. "I think it was just failed attempts and everything else, and I just felt called to powerlifting every time. Before, part of my reluctance was, I think, I associated it with being manly, and I didn't want that. I now see that it's not that at all. I think right now, this is what He wants me to do."

"And we know that in all things God works for the good of those who love Him, who have been called according to His purpose." **Romans 8:28**

But powerlifting had its own unique challenges for Douglas, who at age 8 suffered an autoimmune disease that attacked her pancreas and made her a diabetic. If her sugar is too low, she can't lift. If it's too high, she can't lift, and if her adrenaline gets going from a good lift or two, her body acts like her blood sugar has increased.

"It really does test your patience," Douglas said. "I work very hard to be a controlled diabetic, but it's not easy. It's hard on competition days, because you have to constantly monitor your blood sugar between each lift. I try to use diabetes to glorify God, but sometimes it gets the best of me."

That's one reason why she wears an insulin pump, but usually, she's very self-aware of how her body is reacting. So far, she's met only one other female lifter who is a diabetic.

"But those who hope in the Lord will renew their strength. They

will soar on wings like eagles; they will run and not grow weary,
they will walk and not be faint."
Isaiah 40:31

About a year after she returned to powerlifting, Douglas was
introduced to a man named Ty by a mutual friend, and their
first date was going to a gym for a workout. He's not as avid a
competitor as she is, but he dabbles in bodybuilding, and he is
an avid Christian.

After she won a competition in Huntington, Ind., in March,
Douglas qualified to compete the next month in a world event,
but she'd already had her vacation scheduled for something
else. She and Ty were married June 10. Yes, there was lots of
prayer involved.

Now she's got someone who can help her witness and share
her example of faith with others. One of her favorite quotes is,
"Preach the Gospel at all times. When necessary, use words,"
from St. Francis of Assisi. If the Douglases live up to their own
faith, the opportunities will come.

"But the Lord stood at my side and gave me strength, so that
through me the message might be fully proclaimed and all the
Gentiles might hear it."
2 Timothy 4:17

Now Douglas has personal bests of 352.7 pounds in the squat,
209.4 on the bench and 369.3 on the deadlift, and she ranks
28th nationally in her weight class. Her eventual goals are to be
around 400 on the squat and deadlift and 225 on the bench. If
she reaches those marks, greater opportunities will come.

She's still getting stronger physically, emotionally and also spiritually. She's found exactly where she's supposed to be.

"You can't see what's ahead with your head down, you have to look up," Douglas said. "It's not an easy life, but it's a good one. It's always my goal when I get an opportunity to be God-honoring, and I wouldn't have any of this strength or opportunity without Him. I think if my heart is in it the right way, God will bless me abundantly with strength."

"Have I not commanded you? Be strong and courageous. Do not be afraid; do not be discouraged, for the Lord your God will be with you wherever you go."
Joshua 1:9

CHAPTER 9
There's no slowing the Pfenning family
Published Aug. 30, 2016, in The News-Sentinel

Usain Bolt needs to stick around a few more years, because 10-year-old Zebidiah Pfenning thinks he'll eventually be able to beat the Olympic sprinting king.

Crazy? No crazier than joining a family that adopted four children from four Chinese provinces, or wanting desperately to be a sprinter despite originally missing a left foot and now surviving three surgeries in four years. Or how about winning four gold medals and setting two national records at the Adaptive Sports USA 2016 Nationals while running on a leg that really needed surgery?

Is Pfenning's dream crazier than all of that? Maybe, but if he doesn't catch up with Bolt, his brother Zachariah might provide the challenge. He won two gold medals and a pair of silvers at nationals despite also missing a leg. None of it is more unbelievable than the fact the boys didn't start training until last August and yet won all those medals just last month anyway.

This truly is a unique story. When Mark and Lisa Pfenning got married, they thought they wanted between six and 12 children but found out God had other plans, so they adopted four children from China. Zoe is now 12, Zachariah 11, Zebidiah 10 and Zephira 7 — although she has more energy than the other three combined.

Her mother says Zoe is their child who is differently abled because she doesn't have any physical challenges, but she's the perfect big sister. Zachariah has spina bifida, which led to a left knee amputation. When he was born, his left and right feet were connected and his left leg was six inches shorter. Zebidiah was missing his left foot, and no one knows why. Zephira also has spina bifida and wears braces on both legs, but nothing slows her down. To make things easier, Mom calls them Z1, Z2, Z3 and Z4.

"It's not what we were thinking when we first felt the call," Lisa Pfenning said. "All we knew was these kids needed a home, and two of them were on their last shot. They (Zachariah and Zephira) had been on agency list after agency list, and after a while, they just take you off the list. It has its challenges, and obviously, you are just trying to get through the day."

But there are a ton of smiles each day. The Pfennings are homeschooled through the Indiana Connections Academy, but they were looking for some kind of physical and occupational therapy, so Lisa brings them to Turnstone Center for Children and Adults with Disabilities once a week and has for the last seven years. When they started, Zachariah had just undergone an amputation and back surgery and needed to learn to use a prosthetic leg. Then Zebidiah needed help. About the time Zachariah graduated from his therapy, they brought Zephira home.

As soon as they received their prosthetic legs and learned how to use them, the boys just wanted to run. They'd hurry everywhere and tried a few distance competitions, but what they really needed was a coach and a team to take them in. Turnstone didn't have a team, but Director of Program Outreach Tina Acosta thought she knew where to find a coach.

Brett Freiburger was a Bishop Luers senior in 2001 when a shotgun blast during a hunting accident cost him his left leg after 12 surgeries. Six years later, Freiburger was a nationally ranked sprinter hoping for a chance to compete in the Paralympic Games. Ironically, several people had told him not to even try running in the first place. So seven years after he had stopped competing, he was the perfect coach to work with the Pfennings.

"I want to help them, because I didn't have a lot of the avenues they have," Freiburger said. "They have the drive, so it's easy to coach them. Since they are so young, they are still growing, and getting properly fitting prosthetics is tough, but it's been a fun learning curve with them."

It's been remarkable, actually. After one practice run with the boys, Freiburger told their mother they should be sprinters instead of distance runners. Eight months later, they were winning gold medals at nationals. Along the way, they won a bunch of titles at the Endeavor Games and at Thunder in the Valley in Saginaw, Mich. Despite suffering more pain with each race, Zebidiah kept pushing. When he was finally done with his races, he was ready for another surgery.

His ultimate goal is to become the youngest Paralympian ever at age 14. After that, he just might challenge Bolt.

Considering everything the Pfennings have been through, is the idea really that crazy?

CHAPTER 10
Walter Jordan is still standing up for his beliefs
Published Feb. 18, 2018, on News-Sentinel.com

Last week, a story hit the national wires about San Antonio Spurs coach Gregg Popovich who, concerning the NBA celebrating Black History Month, said, "We live in a racist country. ... And it's always important to bring attention to it, even if it angers some people."

The story hit home for Fort Wayne basketball legend Walter Jordan, who helped Northrop High School win the 1974 state title, became an all-Big Ten player at Purdue University and had a short NBA career.

"I have so much respect for anybody, not just Popovich, who is willing to speak on how he feels and is honest to a fault," Jordan said by phone. "I respect anybody who can do that when it's the right thing to do. It takes serious courage for a man in his position regardless of what someone else is going to think about it."

Jordan's background gives him an interesting perspective on issues. He was part of the first group of black students to be bused from his neighborhood near Central High School to Northrop High School. He always hosted charity games and events in Fort Wayne to help people, and now he lives in Atlanta, where for 14 years, he's run a nonprofit youth summer travel basketball league. He considers it his ministry.

Unlike many today, he doesn't speak in soundbites or read off talking points, and he's not just somebody shooting his mouth off to see who will give him attention. He actually lives the life, mentoring young men every day and hosting yearly leadership conferences. He regularly speaks about topics that interest him on his Facebook page and in public. Sometimes he's blunt and doesn't hold back.

As an example, last year he wrote about how he didn't think it was right for anyone, especially young African-Americans, to use the "N-word" even if it wasn't meant as a derogatory term. It sent the wrong message, he wrote, as if it were acceptable in any form, because that serves to lessen the historical meaning. It should never become even the least bit acceptable or encouraged, he said.

About a year ago, he received a phone call from a mother letting him know her 15-year-old son had been called the slur that day while at school.

"That's the first time?" Jordan responded. "Good."

"What do you mean?" the woman asked.

"Now that we have that out of the way — because eventually, it was going to happen — what are we going to teach him about it? What is he going to learn from this? It's unfortunate, but it's going to happen."

The point was, as Jordan said, there are ignorant people

everywhere. The best things about this world are the people, and sometimes the worst things about this world are the people. Are we going to teach our children to escalate the problems so that maybe they end up in jail or dead, or are we going to teach them how to handle situations so that they can come home safely? There are too many kids and adults who have made horrible 50-second decisions that ended up costing them 50 years of their life.

"It really hurts me when I see how some people, who just complain, don't have a mind of their own and the courage to speak out on things that are wrong," he said last week. "Our kids are watching us! It takes me back to my neighborhood days when we were growing up, and if you were out of line, you were out of line. If someone in your neighborhood saw you doing something wrong, your mom and dad knew about it before you got home."

Over the next few weeks, he's got a trip home planned to watch his first state tournament game since Northrop won in Bloomington in 1974. He's also going to Purdue for a game.

Jordan turned 62 on Monday but says he feels better than ever, because he's working with young people who give him positive energy, respect and hope. He loves talking to them about courage, their dreams and developing their own leadership skills and their own beliefs by listening to the right people.

They are curious, though at the same time trying to understand what's happening and what the adults in the world are doing.

Now he enjoys working with youth more than adults, Jordan said. His parents taught their kids right from wrong, not to care about what others thought of them, to choose love over hate and to stand up for what they believed in. They certainly weren't taught hate, and if he didn't speak up, that's what his parents would be upset about.

Because of the life he has lived, Jordan can speak with authority and conviction. He's not on the outside looking in as a critic, and he also doesn't care if people like what he says, because he'd prefer to be respected for being honestly who he is. He's not looking for approval but to start and continue the conversation he believes we need to have.

"You wouldn't respect me if I didn't say something about those things," he said. "We all have to stand up for what we believe in. We know what's right and wrong, and sometimes it's just about being a decent human being. At the end of the day, if all you can say about me is that I was a pretty good basketball player, I have truly lived an empty, sad and unfulfilled life! I am a product of my environment, my struggles, my victories, defeats, mistakes, experiences and, most importantly, my growth. I am so blessed to have been raised by two of the most loving, God-fearing and wisest people who ever lived (Willie and Laura Jordan)!

"I wish we could stop pointing fingers at each other and sit down and have a decent conversation about what really is God's plan and purpose for all of us."

CHAPTER 11
Afghan vet uses his ability to inspire others
Published Aug. 1, 2015, in The News-Sentinel

Sometimes there are misconceptions about how Ashtan "Five Toes" Wallace lost his left leg. Because he's a former member of the Army National Guard, served in Afghanistan and currently works for the local Veterans Administration, some assume he lost it because of a war injury.

No, and he's quick to correct anyone who suggests that.

His children — Haedyn, 7, and Tatum, 3 — love to tell their friends it's because he didn't eat his vegetables or that a shark bit it off.

Actually, he chose to have it taken off below the knee, but that's jumping ahead a little bit.

In 2008, as a member of the Army National Guard in Nebraska, Wallace was taking a physical training test. He had already passed the pushups and sit-ups portion, but he had to stop the 2-mile run.

"It just felt like knives were stabbing me in the top of the foot on my left side," he said. "I couldn't deal with it anymore. I took off my shoe, and there was a huge bump on top."

The lump was removed and sent in for a test. By the time Wallace returned to have the stitches removed, the doctor told him it was cancerous, a Ewing's sarcoma. Two weeks later, on Christmas Eve, Wallace started chemotherapy and underwent a partial foot amputation on April 10, 2009. He lost everything from his heel forward.

But he didn't lose his dream of serving overseas. He used an ankle brace with a foam pad to fill up his shoe. Training every day, he broke 32 braces in two years.

The National Guard gave him the option of getting out of the service and medically retiring or fighting to stay in.

"I said I wasn't ready to get out, so I had to go through the physicals and all the fun stuff," he said. "I wanted to deploy with my unit."

He eventually passed all the tests, sometimes despite the phantom pain that made it feel like he had a Charley horse in the arch of his left foot, and he hit the ground in Afghanistan with his unit. He took four prosthetics with him and broke them all in 32 days. While duct-taping them together, he tried desperately to get more shipped over but failed. Eventually, he was flown back to Germany and then to San Antonio's Brooke Army Medical Center.

At that point, Wallace decided the situation was not functional and elected to undergo below-the-knee surgery. He promised his wife, Amanda, it would help him become a better husband and father.

"I knew there was a better life at the end of the tunnel," he said. "It hurt at first, but I knew it was going to get better."

He started walking three months later, and three months after that, was playing softball and then wheelchair basketball with a Wounded Warrior team.

Wallace had grown up in Auburn, Ind., and, now 29, moved back with Amanda from San Antonio in February 2012 to start working at SRT Prosthetics and Orthotics as a patient advocate. He also returned to competing. A former high school wrestler, Wallace earned a silver medal at the 2013 Chicago Midwest Valor Games in rowing.

Sports is all about Wallace showing others what he can do without his leg, not what he can't do because of it.

"It made me feel like a human; it made me feel like myself," he said. "When you grow up doing sports and if that gets taken away, just like a limb, you feel a little lost and you don't know what to do.

"If I couldn't do sports or find a way to do (them), I'd probably go a little crazy and would not be a good person to talk to. It gets out a lot of stress. It's your time to be free, to think. Once you know what you are doing, it becomes your hobby, your life, your passion, everything."

That's what he said to his clients at SRT and when he gets the chance now at the VA, where he started in February as a purchasing agent. Sometimes he'll talk to new amputees in the hallway, or maybe a doctor or a nurse will suggest a patient talk to him.

When his foot and then his leg were removed, Wallace had the advantage of being around other amputees, people who suffered horrific injuries who set the example for him, who proved to him that he was not just the result of his amputation. They proved to him that his injury did not and would not define him if he didn't allow it.

Now Wallace encourages the people with new amputations to consider trying sports.

"Any activity or exercise for amputees, even a sit-down sport, is something to stay active and keep the awareness going," he said. "People don't realize there are adaptive sports out there for amputees. It gives you goals and purpose. If you are unable to work, it gives you something to do."

And if they are too depressed by what has happened? If they

are slow to look ahead?

"You've had a fighting spirit before; where's that at? Let's find it, let's dig deep. How do you know what it's going to be like until you try? You aren't going to sit on that chair and give up and go on that powered scooter. You need to get your butt in gear. If we need to go drill sergeant on you, we can do that, but I hate to see you just give up. You have to find something that motivates you — family, kids ..."

Wallace just wanted to deploy with his unit, stand up with and for his buddies, be a good husband and great father, and have a normal life.

Now his goal is to tell others, even those with amputations, they can have that in life, too.

"I just think I have an old soul," Wallace said. "The way I was raised and had to grow up, finding out you have cancer early on gives you a whole new perspective on life. You realize God has a plan, and you can't control it. You just have to make the best of it."

CHAPTER 12
Prayer prepares rookie goalie before each period
Published Nov. 11, 2015, in The News-Sentinel

Before every period of a game, Fort Wayne Komets goaltender Spencer Martin skates to his net and bows his head in prayer. It's a private ritual in a very public profession, but it's also exactly who Martin is. The 20-year-old rookie prays everywhere as a regular part of his life.

"It's something I've been doing for a long time," Martin said. "It's not superstition, it's real. It really puts me in the right spot to play a good game. I'm praying all the time, so it's different stuff. Just, 'Be with me, help me represent you as best I can.' I know whatever his plan is, is the plan, and I'm prepared to go with it. 'Just be with me,' and that's pretty much it."

Martin was raised in a Christian home in Oakville, Ontario. He considers himself an evangelical, born-again Christian, and while many athletes are reluctant to talk about religion, he's happy to talk about his faith with anyone.

"I want to be an influence on and off the ice," he said. "I want to use my hockey platform to be a good role model. You're never going to be perfect, especially in the heat of the battle, but I like to use hockey as a platform to show off my faith. It's real."

To further showcase his faith, Martin has a cross and "PS 118:8" painted on the back of his mask. Psalm 118:8 says, "It is better to trust in the Lord than to put confidence in man." It's also the exact center of the Bible, and Martin uses prayer and that verse to center himself before games and each period.

Besides praying before games, Martin likes taking part in Bible studies. During the summers, he likes to work as an instructor at Hockey Ministries International, which he attended as a child.

"I'm comfortable with everything, people coming to me, meeting new people, and going out and trying to influence anybody I can," Martin said. "And especially learning from others."

He has used Jeremiah 29:11 on the back of two previous masks. It says: "'For I know the plans I have for you,' declares the Lord, 'plans to prosper you and not to harm you, plans to give you hope and a future.'"

"I really use God as a trust thing in games and as a career," Martin said. "You have to trust him in life when you face adversity."

CHAPTER 13
Lamp Lighters keeps providing inspiration
Published July 4, 2017, in The News-Sentinel

Tyler and Ashley Moreland's 2003 Aztek has 250,000 miles on the odometer, a replaced engine, a twice-replaced transmission and barely enough room for two kids along with all the hockey equipment. Though it probably shouldn't, it gets them where they are going.

It's a good example of so many things in the 28-year-olds' lives that probably shouldn't work but always seem to.

Six years ago, they felt inspired to start a street hockey program based on a Christian ministry. They'd teach fundamentals so everyone could have fun, then play games and also offer a small devotion.

Since then, Lamp Lighters Hockey Ministry has worked with more than 800 kids, including Vacation Bible Schools, homeschool gym classes and clinics at eight or nine locations around the county. Every week, the ministry counsels and coaches dozens of kids who can't necessarily afford to play ice hockey.

Something that probably never should have lasted three weeks has a game plan for the future. If anything, the Morelands are more excited today than when they started with no experience, no equipment and no facility but plenty of conviction that they were doing what God wanted.

"It seems like the hardest times have always made things easier because we have learned to trust in God more and more," Ashley said. "It's just doing what we've been called to do. This is the opportunity that God has afforded us, and we're just going to trust that it's all going to happen. If it doesn't work out the way you think it was going to work out, that doesn't mean it wasn't successful, it just means it worked out the way God wanted it to."

In the beginning, they didn't know enough to realize it probably shouldn't work, but somehow they made it happen. Without their faith, no one would have attempted what they are doing, and many friends who started shaking their heads in doubt are now nodding in awe at the way they work.

Somehow, they never seem to get discouraged, even when the Aztek needs more work.

Oh, and with the exception of a small stipend they use to pay for gas, insurance and diapers, the Morelands are volunteer workers. Tyler also is Habitat for Humanity's director of house works, while Ashley stays home with their son and daughter, organizing Lamp Lighters events during naps and after the kids go to bed. There are plenty of challenges, but it's impossible to argue with their success. There have been at least 100 new kids each summer.

"I think the biggest thing I've learned is sometimes you can make a big impact by taking small steps forward, just by saying there's a need, nobody else is doing it and we're just going to keep going," Tyler said. "It's been humbling. If you just put one foot in front of the other and just keep moving, you're going to see that impact over time, even though it may not be what you envisioned in the very beginning."

They've received guidance and help from board members and former Fort Wayne Komets hockey legends like Guy Dupuis, Doug Rigler, Eddie Long, George Drysdale, Kaleigh Schrock, P.C. Drouin, Ron Leef and Nick Boucher, who regularly provide encouragement and make fundraising appearances. Now there are more volunteer coaches and hopes of expanding the program to new churches in the city.

But there have been a few times when the Morelands considered giving up the program, particularly after Tyler's mother passed away in 2015. Their sites were struggling, attendance was dipping and the fundraising was dropping. Realizing an untested faith sometimes doesn't realize its strength, they took time to re-evaluate.

Then good things kept happening and kept them from walking away. Encouraging words came from throughout the city and in hockey. Then they were asked to speak at legendary announcer Bob Chase's funeral service last November. Speaking last, Ashley blew everyone away with her analogy that for years, the Komets broadcaster never got his chance to step up to the NHL, but in his death and faith, he was definitely stepping to the highest level.

"That was a huge motivational shot in the arm for us," Tyler said. "We must be doing something right that we had the opportunity to honor that person, or when another Komets legend steps behind us and says they like what we're doing. There was something inside of us that just said, 'Keep going, keep putting one foot in front of the other, and God has something for us on the other side.' It's still not easy, but it feels better on this side. God continues to keep opening doors for us."

They believe in their purpose with renewed hope and determination. They've seen too many positive taps on the shoulder from God to keep them on the path, and the kids keep coming to play and listen.

"We're not doing anything groundbreaking here, it's just basic stuff," Tyler said. "It's just giving a kid an opportunity that they otherwise wouldn't have. We're here to play hockey, learn about God and have fun. I think people are realizing that Lamp Lighters is not just a flash in the pan. We're committed to the community, and we are not going anywhere."

At least as long as the Aztek keeps moving forward.

CHAPTER 14
Dennis Schebig's Christmas letter
Published in the Bethlehem Lutheran Church Messenger, December 2011

For about five years, I hosted a men's group at Bethlehem Lutheran Church. Longtime Fort Wayne Police Department officer Dennis Schebig was our speaker, and what follows is the story he told, in the form of his annual Christmas letter.

I usually do not take the time or make the effort to write a "Christmas letter." It's not that I don't like them or appreciate those who send them. I have just been too lazy. This year, I decided to send this to you because I feel it is very important to tell you something of a very personal nature. Something that at this Christmas season is really very important to know. More so this year than at any other time of my life.

In April of this year, I had a life-changing experience. One that I feel required to share with everyone I know or meet. I believe that to whom much is given, much is required. Please believe me, much has been given to me. I have been truly blessed.

It was Wednesday, April 23. And it was a beautiful day, but it was still dark as I got out of my bed. I took my shower and shaved like any other day before heading off to work. I kissed Vickie goodbye as I always do and let my big loveable black lab, Bubba, know everything was all right as he laid next to my wife. His tail has a way of telling you he wants you to know you will be missed. It's off to work I go, just like I do every day.

I stopped for my usual breakfast and read the morning paper before heading to my office. Shortly after arriving, I was going through my regular routine of opening things up and getting the warehouse I manage fired up. It's now 7:45 a.m., and I have this horrible pain in my stomach. A very large bulge appeared just above my belt line. I know I need immediate medical help. I was headed to the Emergency Room because after a phone call to my family doctor, Dr. Shelby Kenner, I was told to get there ASAP.

I arrived at the Lutheran Hospital ER about 8:30 a.m. The nurses and the doctor checked me out, and I am soon in la la land. It is amazing what morphine can do to stop the pain. I am told that I have an "incarcerated hernia" and surgery is required. My problem now is I must wait six hours because I had eaten breakfast. I will tell you drugs can be a wonderful thing.

My pastor, Neil Allen, shows up, and thank God he does. He is a very kind and caring person who calms the fears and apprehensions. With him, he brings the peace of Christ. We get through the waiting period and we get to the pre-operating room. It's now 2:30 p.m. As I set up, my surgeon, Dr. Reed, tells me what he will be doing to my body. All of a sudden, my bulge pops back in and the pain goes away. My doctor says we can't put this off. "No, sir!" I reply. I do not want to go through this again.

The operating room is very cold, and I am told I will have a pad placed on my back that will administer my anesthetic. As I lean forward, it is lights out.

What I am going to tell you now is the thing that makes me know my God is real. My God is alive!

My surgeon does a great job. He tells my very worried wife all went well. I am in recovery and doing very good. It is approximately 7:15 p.m.

Over the next 10 to 15 minutes, my life changes completely. It is now 7:30 p.m. Sometime shortly thereafter, my respiration stopped and I quit breathing. My left lung collapsed. A host of doctors are in a very big hurry to get me breathing. There are many tubes and machines and lots of people working very hard to keep me alive. I will be unconscious for the next three days. Vickie took meticulous notes and will fill me in on what happened to me and when as time goes along.

Sometime during that night, my blood pressure will drop to a very low 30/20, and machines are keeping me alive. They have all kinds of bells and whistles going off throughout the night. They breathe for me and monitor everything my body is doing. What they do not do is tell the doctors and nurses that people are praying for me. Good people of many faiths and religions. You see, I know they were because I heard their voices.

I was suddenly in a very bright white room or place. It was the brightest white I have ever seen. Brighter than the sun, yet you did not want to look away from it. I believe it is my Lord and Savior. I cannot tell who is praying for me, but I can hear their prayers. I suddenly reach for this amazing life, and I feel like I touch the hem of my Lord's garment. Just as quickly, I am returned to this world and reality. I wake up, and I am fighting restraints and machines. I am alive!

I am unable to tell you if my journey lasted three seconds, three minutes or three days. You see, in the spiritual realm, time is not a thing that God needs or has use for. Time is something that man has created. I do know that people pray and God hears those prayers. I also know that He does not always answer those prayers in the time frame we would like. Nor does He always say yes to our desires. He may want to think about it for a while. Just like we tell our children, "I don't know, let me think about that." He may want to test us and make sure our faith is in Him. He knows that what we desire may not really be good for us. We have all made the wrong choices at one time or another in our lives. I know I certainly have. There are many things I would do differently if given a second chance.

I am telling you of this experience so that you may know that our God is alive and sits at the right hand of the Father. He hears the prayers of his people. People of many different faiths were praying for me, Jews, Catholics and a whole host of Christian faiths. All of these people are in fact Christ's children.

You ask me how I know, and my answer is this: I was to attend a three-day business meeting in Philadelphia on April 24. Instead of attending the meeting, I became the subject of that meeting. Many of those people have told me they were praying for me (as were) the good people of my church, not to mention my pastor.

I have told this story many times since that day because I believe it is required of me. You see, much has been given to me. A great wife who loves me dearly, outstanding children and grandchildren who I love more than anything.

This is much easier to understand if you are a believer in Jesus Christ. You should know I am praying for you. If you don't believe what I am telling you, then know I am praying for you also! I want you to experience His love and compassion. Just as I have. I want you to know he loves and cares about you just as much as he does me. Christ's grace is unending.

May this Christmas season have extra special blessings for each of you. May the Peace of Christ be with you not only this Christmas but each and every day of the year. This year more than any other, I wish you a Merry Christmas and Happy New Year!

CHAPTER 15
Sue Nation's grace and mercy
Published in the Bethlehem Lutheran Church Messenger, April 2010

In 1993, two men moved into the house next to Jim and Sue Nation because, one of the men told her over the back fence one day, he had come to Indiana to die. He had AIDS and knew his partner would need the support of his family, which was from Fort Wayne.

AIDS was a death sentence back then. It isn't so much now, partly because of the work Sue Nation does with the AIDS Task Force. She has worked as the organization's receptionist and in support services since 2002. She began volunteering with the task force in 1997, shortly after her neighbor died in her living room.

"AIDS is in all areas of society," she says, "no matter what people want to think about it. HIV is something everybody could get."

That's the beginning of the story.

A lifelong nurse until she retired in 2000, Nation was used to dealing with infectious diseases, including stints in Indianapolis and Miami-Dade County, Florida. She was always taught that nurses should be nonjudgmental and should treat everyone, and she often worked with prostitutes and prisoners that were shackled to the beds.

"At the time that HIV came into being in the early 1980s, you wore a gown, mask and gloves, because you didn't know where it was coming from," Nation said. "We didn't know how the disease was being transmitted or how it was coming about."

She was working at Lutheran Hospital in Fort Wayne, when Pat and his partner, Brian, moved in next door.

"Pat's parents had turned their backs on him when he was 5," she said. "They put him in a mental institution in Kentucky because of hyperactivity. Then they moved to California and left him behind."

After having virtually no contact with his family, Pat felt like he was set free when he was released from the institution at age 18. He traveled the country, and that's when he contracted HIV, which developed into AIDS.

During the last 1980s, he ended up in a Cincinnati hospital. The staff there was so afraid they would slide his food tray across the floor. He had to get out of bed, IVs and all, to pick up the tray and place it on the table.

"One night, he was awake when the night shift came in, and one of the nurses said, 'If you want to get out of here alive, you will put your clothes on, go down the back stairs and just walk out, because nobody here will tolerate a gay person, much less one with AIDS. I care for you, but I'm telling you what the whole populace of this hospital is like.'

"So he took out his own IV, put on his clothes, and walked down the back stairs and was gone."

When Pat and Brian moved next door, Jim Nation could relate to the discrimination they were going through because he was confined to a wheelchair. He had suffered a broken neck in 1962 shortly after he got out of the Navy and was paralyzed from the chest down. Eventually, Pat and Brian referred to Sue and Jim as "Mother and Dad."

"When Pat became bedridden, I couldn't help him from my house, so Jim and I moved him into our house, into our living room, in a hospital bed," Sue said. "It was a very tough five weeks."

Pat died in 1996 at age 33 but not before something of a reconciliation with his family, who twice came from California to visit. He also died as a believer and sparked Nation's drive to help fight the disease. She understands how easy it can spread, because before he died, Jim had 57 surgeries, including many, many transfusions.

Sue also had an incident when helping Pat.

"I had given Pat a shot and, for whatever reason, did not put on a pair of gloves," she said. "I hit a blood vessel and he bled all over. All he could do was run and get the Clorox and pour it on my hands. If I had had any cuts on my hands, I'd have been really exposed. After we got the Clorox off, I didn't have any cuts on my hands."

But after Pat died, a hospice worker suggested she be tested anyway.

"That was the most horrifying thing," she said. "Did I want it to be confidential or anonymous? I thought it had to be anonymous. What in the world would my employer think? Nobody could know this.

"I got tested and had to go back in three weeks to get the results. By myself. Now when somebody calls in and they want to know about the testing and the results, I can tell them that I know what it's like to wait those two or three weeks. I understand that panic."

The whole story is a powerful message, especially about how much our perceptions of AIDs and HIV have changed since then.

"I think there's an awful lot we don't know, and we don't need to close our minds to the fact that there are things out there we don't know," Nation said. "People with HIV/AIDS just need somebody to care. I figure on Judgment Day we all have to speak for ourselves, and I have no worry about that."

Imagine if Jesus had turned his back on the lepers, the prostitutes … or us.

CHAPTER 16
'Miracle' Olympian Wells holds hope despite health issues
Published Feb. 21, 2015, in The News-Sentinel

How desperate would someone have to become to sell his or her Olympic gold medal, something he or she had sacrificed everything for, even the chance to make a fortune as a professional? What could happen to crush hope that much?

For many of his teammates on the 1980 United States Olympic hockey team, Mark Wells, 57, is the player who disappeared. He stopped playing in 1981 after 19 games with the Fort Wayne Komets and went home to St. Clair Shores, Mich., figuring he'd already seen the ultimate in his hockey career and wondering whether the same was true of his life.

After he made the hockey team at Bowling Green State University as a walk-on and then survived the cuts to make the national team, Wells was continually manipulated by coach Herb Brooks before the Olympics. He was used as the example for the rest of the team, several times getting shipped out to minor league teams. He even overcame a broken ankle before being recalled the week before the Olympics, the last man named to a team that made history.

Though as a center he'd scored a ridiculous 232 points in 154 college games, Wells was asked by Brooks to concentrate on defense. Wells scored two goals and played a vital fourth-line role in the Olympics, probably playing more minutes than anyone against the Russians.

"My mission was to shut down the other team's top line, and I did my job," Wells said. "I was like the shadow, and I shut down everybody. I was the only guy walking around the Olympic Village telling everyone we were going to win. Everybody said, 'But you just lost to the Russians 10-3!' But I hadn't played that game."

And then he laughed.

During the tournament, he backed up his confidence. Opponents never scored a goal while he was on the ice, and at the end, he proved his worth and celebrated with his teammates. After a trip to the White House and a quick celebration back home, Wells played the next year with New Haven of the American Hockey League before bouncing around Oklahoma City; Flint, Mich.; and finally Fort Wayne, Ind.

"Montreal had traded my rights after the Olympics, and I was disheartened and lost my enthusiasm and drive," Wells said. "I had always dreamed of playing with the Canadiens. I'd had a great hockey career and had experienced one of the greatest moments of all time."

He went home to help a buddy run a restaurant but wrenched his back while moving some produce. After not missing a day of work in five years, Wells had to be carried out of the restaurant and faced immediate surgery. Though doctors didn't realize it at the time, he had a genetic spinal degenerative disc disorder. The first surgery lasted 12 hours, and afterward, doctors told him the damage was more extensive than expected.

He spent three years bedridden inside a body cast hoping the vertebrae would fuse, but then another surgery revealed the screws had broken off. That meant three more years in a body cast. This time, doctors prescribed heroin for the pain, but eventually even that failed, so Wells tried OxyContin and nerve blocks.

"I started to feel extreme pain to the point of suicide," he said. "My spirits kept falling, and I said, 'My life is over. I'll never have a wife or kids.' I was in so much pain that nothing mattered to me. I had no idea how to survive or exist."

In all, Wells spent nine years in a body cast, was declared disabled, and in 2002, sold his medal for $40,000 to help pay the bills. It later sold at an auction for more than $300,000.

How did he survive? He couldn't rely on anything but faith.

"I have an athlete's mentality of toughness and hope, and that helped me to be a powerful, spiritual person to fight this disease," he said. "I have God all over my room, and Mother Mary. I read about the Spirit that said, 'I will see you one day, my son, in a better place.' I pray every day to make a little bit of progress."

Though Wells also suffered a stroke in March 2013, he recovered and faces more surgery. Still, some positive things are finally starting to happen. Wells and his partner, Tonia Flenna, have two boys, ages 5 and 2. St. Clair Shores, Mich., renamed the municipal rink in his honor last year. And he's looking forward to this weekend's reunion in Lake Placid, N.Y., with his former teammates.

"All the guys have known I've suffered with this," he said. "It's going to be amazing to see them and know that we were legends at such a young age. This thing grew beyond anything we ever dreamed of, and it will be here for 285 years, not just 35. None of us realized the importance this would have on society still today."

On March 4, there will be another surgery, his sixth, and maybe another in the future, but Wells thinks he has found a surgeon who is as tough as he is. Recovery will take a year, and Wells will sleep in a lift chair for at least three months. Three months? That's nothing, he said.

"I have high hopes and very big plans," he said. "After the dedication of the rink, I have to do it. It has given me an opportunity, a hope of inspiring all the youth players in St. Clair Shores. They are witnessing a man who has done it, and my focus is on those youth now. It gives me hope to build a larger foundation."

Finally, Mark Wells has a flicker of hope again.

CHAPTER 17
Walleye captain survives, thrives after health crisis
Published May 2, 2017, in The News-Sentinel

The first time Alden Hirschfeld suffered a grand mal seizure, he was sleeping, and his spasms terrified his wife Lauren, who was eight months pregnant with their first child. He had no idea what was happening, or even if he was possibly dying.
Caused by abnormal electrical activity in the brain, the seizure includes violent muscle contractions and a loss of consciousness. The results can last from 10 seconds to usually under two minutes. There are all kinds of horrible symptoms, and wondering when and if the next one will hit or what will trigger it is probably the worst consequence, the unspeakable fear.

Randomly, the Toledo Walleye hockey forward from Sylvania, Ohio, suffered two more seizures, again both while sleeping.

Doctors believed they knew what was wrong and prescribed medication, which helped somewhat. A defensively responsible, gritty player who doesn't make many mistakes, Hirschfeld continued to play very effectively and was even called up to play for Grand Rapids of the American Hockey League for the third year in a row. The Griffins were informed of his medical condition.

"I'd had my eyes checked, and different CT (computerized tomography) scans and tests and angiograms, everything done that you need to do," Hirschfeld said. "The doctors all saw the same spot, but we were just trying to monitor it and try to let the medicine work."

But on Jan. 8, 2016, during the second period of a Grand Rapids home game against Milwaukee, Hirschfeld was sitting on the bench when he suffered his fourth seizure. Unresponsive, he was carried to the locker room as panic spread throughout Van Andel Arena.

"The guy means so much to us," Griffins broadcaster Bob Kaser said. "The emotions were awful. He loves the game of hockey and loves to play. Everybody just thinks the world of him because he's one of those guys who automatically people are drawn to."

As scary as the medical emergency was, it might have been a blessing, at least that's how Hirschfeld came to look at it. Because the Griffins are the farm team of the Detroit Red Wings, the organization was able to find him the best specialists to study the problem and who just happened to work in Grand Rapids. In an odd way, having a seizure during a game helped bring necessary attention to his situation.

"I got the right help, for sure," he said. "I think part of it was about wanting to keep playing. I had some people say no, and others say yes. Detroit said I wasn't going to be able to play the rest of the year, so I thought I'd take the opportunity to get different opinions and see what everybody is going with. The main thing was about getting better away from hockey, being a dad and a husband. I wanted to do what I felt was best for the future and the long term. Let's try and get this taken care of and be done with it."

Doctors diagnosed him with a cavernous malformation in the temporal lobe behind his left eye, and on March 14, he underwent a craniotomy, a lengthy surgery which opened his skull to remove a tangle of muscles, veins and arteries about the size of a fingertip.

Within a few months, Hirschfeld was cleared to skate again, and just before training camp, he received permission to take part in full-contact drills.

"It was tough to get it all figured out, but when you trust in the Lord and have good faith in Him and know that He has a plan, you let Him lead you and guide you," Hirschfeld said. "Everything has been positive since. It was a tough half a year there to get through it all and deal with it, but being able to play again and do what I love has been pretty special."

There have been no more problems, and Hirschfeld easily produced the best season of his five-year career with 23 goals and 49 points in 55 games. Even better, on Feb. 15, he was named captain of the Walleye.

"He has a determination and a will to succeed not only in hockey but also in life," Walleye broadcaster Matt Melzak said.

"What he has gone through the last year, to see him announced as captain was a thrill for me after getting to know him the last couple of years, and I'm sure it was a thrill for him as well. I think the players were all very happy to see him as captain."

As Kaser said, "He's got a lot to accomplish in life and a lot of people to bless with his presence. He's just an exceptional human being. He's easy to root for in all forms of life. There's been nothing more gratifying than to see him recover from a health standpoint and be able to be that awesome father and fantastic husband and great friend to so many people, and also to be able to play again the game that he loves."

Off the ice, it's also been a remarkable year for Hirschfeld. Daughter Vivian is now 2 1/2, and is expecting a baby brother or sister within the next month. Besides leading the Walleye to the ECHL's best record, her dad has also made time to speak with young patients who are facing some of the same things he has. He rarely thinks about what he's been through, just happy to live a blessed life and play hockey.

"It's just been unbelievable, very special, one of those things where you know everything happens for a reason," he said. "It's happened and been fixed at the right time, and now hopefully I'm good to go. I'm just happy things have gone the way they have and super blessed to be back on the ice doing what I love to do. It's always fun to do what you love to do."

Maybe, he wonders, if God didn't have him go through this experience to use him as an example for others later. He's not arguing, because there's nothing left to be afraid of.

"You just have to trust in the Lord and His plan, and that's what we're going to do."

CHAPTER 18
Somer Johnson becoming spiritual and emotional leader

Published Sept. 30, 2016, in The News-Sentinel

Somer Johnson is not only one of the best players on the Indiana University-Purdue University Fort Wayne volleyball team, she's one of its best people. The Snider High School graduate sees her four-year journey as a psychology major at IPFW as part of a spiritual trek. That's how she sees playing for a team and why she's hosting a Bible study for the IPFW Volleydons.

"I've always been part of the church at Blackhawk Christian, but my freshman and sophomore year, I was on and off going to church," Johnson said. "I kind of felt drawn away, and this year specifically I felt more drawn to it."

She started dating Jedidiah Davis about a year ago, and he helped pull her back into the church. She made the decision to get baptized in May.

"My New Year's resolution this year was to be a better Christian, do more good and be more involved," she said. "I felt like this was my chance at kind of a fresh start. I felt compelled to write and give my testimony to try to inspire someone else out there by talking about my journey and what I've been going through."

As part of her decision to live her life for God, Johnson decided to host a Bible study for her teammates. College athletes are already very busy maintaining academic and practice schedules, but Johnson felt inspired to offer something different.

"I was definitely nervous about it," she said. "Do I really know that much about it to teach these other girls? Do I know what to say? I've been thinking about it over the summer, so it was in the back of my mind. I prayed about it and talked to Jed and my family about it, and I felt like I was being called to do it, even though it's not inside my comfort zone."

She sent out a group message, and four teammates showed up the first time. Now, between four and six are meeting each week. Johnson leads the discussion but tries to tailor it to help fit a group of young women who also are athletes. They talk about things going on in their lives, concepts that fit both the team and faith, and how they can use spiritual ideas to grow as teammates. She tries to help show how faith can affect their everyday lives.

As an example, they've studied concepts such as integrity, work ethic and loyalty.

"This is truly a passion of hers," Volleydons coach Steve Florio said. "We have a good contingent of players who are very strong in their faith, and Somer is about as good a person as you are going to meet in life. We're not a Christian school, but the values on our team lean in that direction pretty hard. We do a lot of service, and it's the culture on the team right now. Our team is a very strong group of people and not all strong in their faith, but they are all good people."

There also is respect for those of other faiths on the team.

Johnson said she may hold sessions during downtime on road trips. She's interested in working with Fellowship of Christian Athletes and trying to take advantage in other ways of her renewed faithful energy.

"I just want to inspire them to follow Jesus," she said, simply. "I don't necessarily want to be remembered for what I did on the court, but more so for who I was off the court. I want this year to be more about not being upset by wins and losses. I obviously want to win a championship because we haven't had one for a while. I want a winning year, but there are a lot more things out there that are important. I'm playing for my team and for God's glory and not my own."

CHAPTER 19
DeDee Nathan answers the call
Published June 10, 2004, in The News-Sentinel

The equipment was packed away, the medals dusted and the schoolbooks purchased. As far as DeDee Nathan was concerned, her athletic career was over. It was January 2003, and finally, after 23 years of competing, it was time to get on with the rest of her life.

Except she forgot to check with the most important person in her life. Nathan was at a prayer meeting in Bloomington, Ind., when she got the message she really didn't want to hear.

"As the pastor was getting our prayer requests, his wife went around and prayed over each of us," Nathan said. "When she got to me, she said, 'The Lord said go back, you aren't done yet.'"

Nathan was not happy. In fact, the reason she hadn't prayed about her decision before was because she had accomplished her goal of making an Olympic team and did not think there was anything left that needed to be done as far as her track-and-field career was concerned. She was 35, after all, and that's usually past the prime of any athlete, let alone a world-class competitor in the heptathlon.

"I was enjoying life, being able to go to class and then go home," she said. "I've learned to be obedient even if I don't want to do it. The point is I'm being obedient and whatever happens, happens."

So Nathan called all her old coaches and started running and lifting weights again.

"She said she had to do this no matter what," coach George Freeman said. "I think this is a good way for her to end."

Luckily, Nathan had about one year to get back into shape in time for the Olympic Trials on July 9-10 in Sacramento, Calif. She had just the right amount of time left to make it work. Because she was a veteran, she knew exactly what and how much she had to do. She knew her body.

"The understanding of the preparation and of one's workout indicators, which confirm a certain level of performance capability, is something only veterans are capable of understanding and meeting," said Greg Harger, coach of the Indiana Invaders. "If anyone can pull off (making) another Olympic team under the circumstances DeDee faces, it is DeDee. She has the professional temperament to make this a reality."

Physically, Nathan said she feels fine. If anything, taking the time away allowed her body to regain full strength for her comeback. As a veteran, she knows not to overtrain and that sometimes pushing is the wrong thing to do.

She hasn't competed in a meet as of yet, but she "feels" her performance is where it needs to be at this time. She's on pace to peak during the trials. Her times are dropping and distances improving each week.

"I didn't lose my love for the sport," she said. "It was just enough. At this point, it's not about having the passion, it's about being obedient to God. I've learned over the past 13 years of being a Christian that being obedient is better than sacrifice.

"God is real to me and my life, and if he told me to go out there and run for whatever reason, I'm going to go out there and do it."

But without that personal fire, can she find the enjoyment she needs to be at her best? Nathan believes her calmness is an advantage. She has been there, done that, for three previous Olympic Trials, making the team in 2000. She won't be nervous or even uptight. She'll be cool under fire.

"That's just my personality," she said. "You are going to do what you are going to do, and ultimately, all you can do is do your best on those two days. That's it."
The finality of her statement sounds not so much like acceptance as uncertainty, though she was confident there was a purpose to her return to training. After 23 years of competition and 13 years as a Christian, she had learned that what is meant to happen in spite of preparation and athletic ability will happen.

"You just never know what's going to happen. My thinking is, I want to be (as) prepared as possible to do the best I can do. Whatever happens, happens."

Her coaches have been looking for that mental edge to go with the physical.

"I think she's going to be competitive, and at first I wasn't sure," Freeman said. "She wasn't prepared for it. It takes some mental aspect. The one good thing is that she feels like an underdog this time, and she likes that."

Nathan figures God will give her that fire, especially if he has a purpose for this comeback.

"My gift has made room for me, as the Bible says," she said. "I'd like to complete things and move on. Maybe there's a medal there, but God really does know. He would definitely have to bless me and help me physically to get it done."

NOTE: Following God's path for her, Nathan finished fifth in the 2004 trials and did not qualify for her second Olympics in Athens. She hung up her spikes to start her career as a teacher and school administrator in Indianapolis. As for the purpose of her second attempt at the Olympics?

"You never know if you may have said something small to someone that might make a difference later," she said.
Or when such obedience might prove to be an inspiration to other Christians.

CHAPTER 20
Wichman-Jones found higher purpose after gold medal
Published May 20, 1997, in The News-Sentinel

Imagine you're 16 years old and you've achieved what many would consider the peak moment of any life — winning a gold medal at the Olympics.

"For about a year, my world was wonderful," remembered Sharon Wichman-Jones, who won the 200-meter breaststroke at the 1968 Mexico City Olympics as a Snider High School junior. "I gave a lot of talks. People were so excited back then that I would tell them, when they asked me to speak, that I could do a Q-and-A. They'd ask questions for two hours. That keeps you going and excited."

Eventually, practicing became harder and harder. After sacrificing so much to make the Olympics, Wichman-Jones didn't feel the drive to continue swimming with her major goal already accomplished, and she quit after two more years.

"I didn't realize how (goal-oriented) I was until I tried to swim afterward," she said. "I had already done the only thing I ever wanted to do in swimming. Just to swim for swimming sake was not what I wanted to achieve the rest of my life."

But she wasn't really sure what the rest of her life was supposed to be about, so she drifted. She never dropped out of society or became a delinquent, but she wondered if the best days of her life were passed. Along the way, she worked at the Fort Wayne Children's Zoo, married David Jones in 1973 and delivered their first son, Carter, in 1975.

David eventually went to Purdue University to finish his degree while Sharon coached an AAU swimming team. They came home to Churubusco, Ind., in 1978. David's father bought Jones Hydroponics in 1980 and put David and Sharon in charge. Shortly after, a second son, Logan, was born.

It was a full life, but not a totally fulfilling one. Sharon tried coaching off and on but disliked leaving her family at night. She began working in the office of the family business and driving a school bus for Northwest Allen County Schools. She was still looking for something, but she didn't know what.

"I wanted to try to find something I was good at so I could excel in another area, but I couldn't find anything (that) I could be great at so people would admire me anymore," she said. "I had done everything in my life that I thought could possibly make me happy — I went to the Olympics, got married and had kids, but the highs only lasted a little while. There was a deep void, an absence in my life. I went to the church because I knew that was where the answer was going to be."

Twelve years ago, Wichman-Jones became a born-again Christian. Now her life has the stability she had been searching for, and a goal that she says is higher than going to the Olympics. The realization changed her life.

"What I had to realize in my faith and walk with the Lord (was that) he no longer wanted me to look great; he wanted me to make him look great," she said. "There isn't anything you (can) achieve in this world that's great by the world's standards that has meaning for very long. You think that the things the world has to offer will fulfill you, but they don't for very long. The only thing that lasts is to know God and to serve him."

Now she often speaks to groups ranging from 6-year-olds to senior citizens. She tells them how she started as a swimmer and what it was like to be an Olympian.

"One of the things that made me go in the direction of swimming was that a lot of my friends were starting to do things they shouldn't be doing, and I didn't want to do that, so I poured myself into swimming and school," Wichman-Jones said. "Then I started telling them about my relationship with Jesus Christ. I know where I'm going, and I just wish more people could see the truth."

She also talks about the Olympics today, telling the children to be the best they can be, not the best the performance-enhancing drugs can make them. Like everyone else, she watched the Olympics last summer as a fan, though she does have a unique perspective.

"When you look at it on TV, it seems pretty much the same," she said. "I still get a charge out of watching them compete. I like to see the reaction of the swimmers after the race is over. I cried. The first thing you think when you're done is all that hard work was worth it. It brings back all the memories."

CHAPTER 21
Carol Booker learned God's patience
Published in the Bethlehem Lutheran Church Messenger, December 2009

We've all heard people say, "In His way and in His time," but how many of us actually have the courage to believe it? Saying we have the faith is easy, but actually waiting until that time comes is often a lot harder – like almost impossible!

Carol Booker has lived through a couple of examples that will blow you away.

You may know her as the wife of Earl and mother to Jason, Lia, Nathan and Julia. She also has seven grandchildren ranging in age from 3 to 16, and she's been a member of Cross Connections for the past two years. She's also the unofficial Bethlehem Lutheran Church nurse, which means she'll check in on people when asked by church leaders to give suggestions on health issues. She hopes to see that portion of her lay ministry expand soon.

Carol and Earl grew up in southern Indiana and have been married for 38 years. When they had been married for about two years, the Bookers moved to Fort Wayne, where Carol started taking nursing classes. The Bookers came to Bethlehem from Zion in the early 1980s.

Carol's faith soon faced a major test because of some things she had experienced growing up. She had come from an abusive home, and a lot of those memories started sneaking up on her.

"I kind of went off the deep end, and I moved away from God," she said. "For probably three years, I never stopped believing in God, but ..."

She ignored Him?

"No, I just thought He was out to get me!"
That's a pretty heavy issue, but about five years ago, a friend suggested she try a new counselor at Bethlehem named Terrie Ensley. With her patience, Terrie was able to tremendously help Carol, who said the counseling was a blessing.

"I told Pastor Olsen once, 'Some people come to the Lord real gently, and some of us come kicking and screaming,'" Carol said. "I've always been a kicker and a screamer. It really just hit me. From then on, it was like I didn't question Him. I stopped viewing God as being out to get me but as a father. He couldn't just tap me to get my attention.

"I've been fortunate enough to actually see miracles in my life that had no explanation other than God."

God had a couple more taps coming her way, and the first time, he put away the two-by-four and went for the hammer. In September 2004, Carol started getting ill, suffering nausea that led to her losing 120 pounds in a year. No one could tell her what was wrong.

"Everybody thought I was going to die," she said.

She finally ended up at the Indiana University Medical Center, where doctors suggested stomach surgery, though they said they weren't sure if that would work because they still had no idea what was wrong. On the 3 1/2-hour drive home from the center, Carol finally figured something out: Everyone's first inclination is to fight through things themselves, even when they don't have to.

"It just finally dawned on me that God was really trying to get my attention," she said. "I just knew this was God tapping me on the shoulder saying, 'Will you pay attention to me now?' He was trying to tell me something. I made changes in my diet that the doctors had not recommended, and within about two months, I was feeling a lot better."

Part of the changes included getting involved with Cross Connections where she specializes in anxiety and depression. Still to this day, the doctors can't tell her what was wrong, but there have been no relapses.

"I just know it was God trying to tell me something," she said. "I think it was just God's way of saying, 'Take my hand. Don't do this by yourself.' So I did."

That's not a regular prescription, but it works, and Carol now has that connection of experience she can share with her covenant partners in Cross Connections.

"I always believed, but never for myself," she said. "I think it was because of my childhood. I was told for as long as I could remember that I was no good. That I was bad. My father was a terrible alcoholic. He struggled, and I caught the brunt of it. Everything was my fault. It never occurred to me not to believe, but I always believed for everybody else."

Maybe that's something along the lines of how it's easier to forgive someone than it is to ask for forgiveness. It's also easier to pray for others sometimes, asking God to give them help, than it is to pray for ourselves and ask Him to help us.

"If it came back tomorrow, I'd say, 'OK, what did I miss?'" she said. "I wouldn't wait to be so ill this time. There was no other answer."

Believe it or not, that experience helped her through another problem shortly after that. Carol and Earl had been attempting to raise their first grandson who had been diagnosed with all kinds of problems. It was causing incredible strain in their lives, and the boy was in and out of institutions. They knew what he really needed was parents. Eventually, they went to talk to an attorney who specialized in older children with special needs and adoption. He told them he didn't think he could help.

"We finally said to God, 'Take him,'" Carol said. "I didn't mean take him home, but I meant take him. God just said, 'Keep doing what you are doing. I will not forsake you, I will not forsake him.' That always kept coming back to me."

After the meeting with the attorney, Carol went to dinner with four former co-workers and told them about the problems. One of the women said she worked with someone who had adopted a daughter and also a baby boy that had recently died. The next morning the wife, who happened to be an advocate for children with special needs, called, and that night, the Bookers and the couple got together to talk for hours. The couple met the grandson and immediately fell in love with him. They called the attorney back, and the grandson was adopted.

"It is the hand of God," Carol said. "He's on no medicine and he's top of his class now, he is very active in his church youth group and we get to be grandparents again. It is the hand of God. When people say God doesn't do anything, I go, 'Oh, yes, he does.' Why did it take so long? I have no idea."

The grandson is 13 now, and that incident took place four years ago.

That may be an extreme example of giving up control of a situation to God.
"I didn't do that early," Carol said. "I kept thinking I had to fix it. To be able to give that up ... I would not have been able to do that if I hadn't had the prior illness and (learned) to let God handle it. I still would have been struggling. We were back in a corner, and we didn't feel there were any good options. When they say 'In God's time,' they mean that.

"When I sit and I don't have anything else to do, I can make a list of the blessings that we've received, that I have received just since I learned to listen to God. Some people can't see their blessings, but so many times now, I can see them. Many times, something happens and you are blessed, but you don't realize it. It takes a sequence of events for you to see the hand of God again."

CHAPTER 22
Elvis Netterville never gives up on anyone
Published in the Bethlehem Lutheran Church Messenger,
August 2007

While visiting the Bethlehem Lutheran Church office one afternoon a couple of years ago, Elvis Netterville picked up a letter with a return address from the Allen County Jail. It essentially said, "You were right, and I should have listened."

Netterville shook his head that day — and then went to meet the young man to try again.

The young man was not a member of Bethlehem, but to whom else should he have written? The real question is to whom else could he have written, because had there been someone else, he might not have been involved in those circumstances. He had no one else, but he knew Netterville wouldn't give up on him.

Netterville never gives up on anybody.

The need for positive male role models is one reason why he developed Christian Urban Ministries 12 years ago as part of his mission as Bethlehem's Missionary to Southeast Fort Wayne. One of his main focuses is providing an example of a positive male role model for the boys in the area, many of whom are poor and come from single-parent households headed by a woman.

"It's always surprising how they respond to that positive encouragement, from the little guys all the way up to the big guys," Netterville said. "We tell these kids we love them. That's something they don't hear much. I've told kids, 'I don't know what your image of yourself is, but over the next semester, I want you to trust me and you see yourself as I see you, because I'm way closer to being right than you are. I see you like God sees you.' Some guys have never heard that."

The most successful aspect of the ministry is the basketball program, which runs year-round on Tuesdays, Wednesdays and Thursdays.

Basketball is just the primary tool, not necessarily the primary focus. The program uses the boys' interest in basketball to encourage development in other areas. Goals are established for conduct on the gym floor, in the classroom, in the community and in their relationship with God. They are not allowed to play if there are any grades below a C, but participants are given encouragement and sometimes study help to improve their grades. It may be unconventional, but the program works, sometimes starting with something as simple as making a big deal out of an F grade improving to a D.

"The things that have been the most successful have been the things the Lord has shown us how to do," Netterville said.

There have been attempts to hire tutors, but Netterville says anecdotal evidence has shown the same results when tutors are not used. Mostly, all the students need is encouragement and expectations, maybe as easy as someone to care and express an interest in how they are doing. Then the students make the changes.

"We know that when we put a well-behaved child with expectations in the school system, they can be taught," Netterville said. "We can't do that as well as the school system can, but we can help the boys develop the desire to learn."

"I have not had to help many kids. It's amazing what they can do when they pay attention and want to do it. Usually, what happens is they take care of it themselves. They get in to see the counselors and do what they need to do."

The players also are encouraged to go to church with a parent, a grandparent or even one of the three coaches: Netterville, Ed Ramos or Willie Shears. Besides coaching, they provide an example of how a man is supposed to act in his work, in play and in church.

This fall, the goal for the overall grade point average for the four middle school teams is a B, compared to their current grade point averages of a D or below. Netterville says the grade point averages of the participants in the program are substantially higher than they are for those outside the program who are facing the same circumstances. The system attracts the students because it starts with basketball.

"A lot of folks don't get it about basketball," Netterville said. "This is a very powerful tool for this community. We start with basketball, and we do ministry with them, it just all starts with basketball. This draws them in and gets them focused on something they want to be good at. Once they decide they want to be good at something, then they can be good at a lot of things."

Kids in the program do not get in trouble in school. If they do, Netterville or one of the coaches will visit the school, with the parent's permission, and discuss the situation with the student and teachers. Usually, the threat is enough, because the students do not want to let the coaches down.

Though he's been too busy to gather statistics, Netterville said there's been an incredible decrease in the number of students who end up in jail, and the number who go to college is starting to rise. Now they are the ones starting to provide the examples of what could happen if a student gives the program, and himself, a chance.

The program is obviously a success, except in one way, an area in which Netterville has possibly just been too busy to fix. They need more people to get involved, especially members from Bethlehem. The church hosts the program but is not much a part of it.

"Where we have a lot more work to do is telling the story in a way that we get many more people to participate in it," he said. "One of the things that comes out of it is they will absolutely be blessed by it. There's no doubt about it. When you love these kids, then you'll see 20 streams of love coming back at you. It's one of the most rewarding things you can go through. There's an opportunity here to really have a huge impact on kids' lives, and you will be blessed by it."

That doesn't mean the program needs more basketball coaches or referees. Sometimes it means just being an option for one of the students to talk to. One of the program's situations is that many of the students do not attend Bethlehem, but Netterville believes they would if more Bethlehem members showed a genuine interest in them. Maybe it includes going with Netterville on a visit.

"You have to understand that it is the Holy Spirit working and it's about love," Netterville said. "It's the most miraculous thing I've ever seen. Love cuts through all these barriers like a hot butter knife. It's not going to take you weeks, I'm talking about minutes. People know when you like them. That's all you have to do. We all know how to treat people that we like. What makes it work is love, and we already know how to love people. That and the Holy Spirit will remind us that we are representing Jesus Christ. People will see it in our smiles and in how we treat them."

Maybe that means something as simple as not giving up on someone, even when they might be in jail. Netterville said he has never written a kid off, but when they write to him, it's just another chance to get through to them. Maybe then they'll just be more willing to listen.

"Usually, you are telling a kid, 'You really made a bad choice. Understand that I still love you, but this was a mistake.' You just have to give them the idea that when they come out … they are not going to be cast off."

And isn't providing another chance the true work of all missionaries?

CHAPTER 23
God finally got through to Ed Ramos
Published in the Bethlehem Lutheran Church Messenger, August 2007

No matter how far a person slides, God can always jerk the chain and bring one of his children back. For Bethlehem Lutheran Church elder Ed Ramos, the chain God used was just a pager.

Ramos says that now he's a very simple guy, but in the past, he led a very complicated life.

"My life hasn't always been real bright, but it is now," he said. "It was ugly, but the last seven years have been very good."

A 1982 South Side High School graduate, Ramos served six years as a United States Army infantryman and combat MP before starting work at Holsum Bakery for 13 years. Then, after his mother and father passed away within six months of each other, Ramos admits, "I went off on my own for a while."

Ramos drank heavily and lived as a homeless person. For three or four years, he'd do the odd maintenance job, mow grass, shovel snow or whatever he could find to earn a little money. Then he'd go to a bar, where a beer cost a buck and sometimes less on special days.

Once in a while, he'd stay with one of his five sisters or sometimes with friends, and other times, he'd live out of a beat-up brown Ford van. One night as he slept off a drinking binge, his van was spray-painted, but he never heard a thing. A couple of times, he got pulled over and sent to jail for drunk driving.

Often, he'd wash up in a McDonald's. Other times, there were friends who would feed him, let him shower and do his laundry.

He still had his faith, but he didn't practice it. Occasionally, he'd walk into his childhood church, St. Patrick's Catholic, and light a candle. Sometimes, he'd say a prayer for ex-wife Sue and his three children, while other times, he'd just sit and look around. He was physically there but not mentally there, though he knew something was pulling him back.

The one thing that kept him grounded was a pager, but he still can't figure out how it stayed active. He kept fresh batteries in it but never paid the service for it. Usually, it was one of his sisters calling to see what he was doing, and sometimes it was Sue checking in. He'd often call from a bar that night.

One day, he got a call from Sue, and when he called back that night, his daughter Christina asked him to come to her Easter program at Bethlehem. A few weeks later, she called again to tell him her confirmation was coming up. That led to a meeting with Sue and Pastor Gregory Manning that helped change Ed's life. From that point on, he started coming to Bethlehem.

"I just got sick of being drunk," he said. "I was tired of being drunk and tired of not knowing what was going on with the kids or being around them. I guess I finally realized it was time to grow up."

Pastor Tom Eggold invited him to Bible class, and Ramos started going all the time. Eventually, for the first time in his life, he started going to church by himself. He gave his testimony to a couple of Bible classes, and he's been sober since 2001.

"Whenever I smell smoke, sometimes I'll remember those times, and I go get a pack of gum or a cold Diet Pepsi, and I'm good to go," Ramos said.

Now Ramos works at Hospital Laundry Services as a maintenance man, helps with Christian Urban Ministries and is an elder working with the board of outreach. He also serves breakfast every Saturday and Sunday at the Fort Wayne Rescue Mission.

When he sees a counseling opportunity, he'll tell people he's been there. He's seen the darkness and the ugliness. He's survived it.

"Sometimes I'll see one of my old buddies over at the mission," he said. "I know where they are at, and I know where I could be at if I didn't get my life straightened out. I'll go over and sit and talk with them, because you never want to feel that you think you are better than they are. I don't know if it is giving back. It's more that I was there, and I know where you're at, and I can help show you how to get some help."

Ed Ramos has a story of redemption, and he understands God doesn't let you get too far away. Now Bethlehem has become his sanctuary, and he's an example to all of us that you can always come back.

CHAPTER 24
Shelby Gruss rebuilt her life on faith
Published June 24, 2013, in The News-Sentinel

While lying in the hospital, trying to somehow comprehend her paralysis from the waist down, Shelby Gruss first understood she wasn't alone.

"God was always there for me. From the start, he had a lot to do with me just saying, 'OK, this is how it's going to be the rest of the way.' I had a strong base with God before it happened, and honestly, I don't think I would have had such a good attitude in the hospital without that."

It seems like yesterday to many, but it's been more than three years since Gruss was an 18-year-old Bishop Luers High School senior attempting a big air jump while snowboarding during Christmas break in Ohio. The board flipped from under her, and she landed on her shoulder and upper back, breaking the T8 and dislocating the T9 vertebrae.

We all dread the unknown of change. Every time Facebook adds a tweak, the major result is mass complaining. A great new idea at work usually results in anxiety. Everyone tenses at road construction and the disruption of routine.

Gruss had to deal with one of the largest changes possible. Her existence flipped over as much as the snowboard that had been providing her base. Not only was her basketball season finished, but so were all the other plans she had for the rest of her life. Everything changed except her faith and her attitude.

"God takes special people to do that, because not everybody could have handled it the way she does," Bishop Luers basketball coach Denny Renier said. "It's just hard to believe I could have handled it the way she has when you look at the devastation and the chances you may be in that chair the rest of your life, and she's been that way from Day One."

This fall, Gruss will start attending the University of Illinois to study crop science and play on the wheelchair basketball team. She doesn't consider herself an inspiration, but if others want to look at her that way, that's OK, too.

"I just think I'm a normal person going through everyday life," she said. "If I inspire people, that's OK."

The inspiration started almost immediately. Everyone who visited expected the worst, but Gruss cheered them up.

"I can tell you from when I went to see her in the hospital, it was more upsetting for me than it was for her," longtime Bishop Luers athletic department secretary Joni Kuhn said. "She comes whipping down the hall in that wheelchair with a big smile on her face, and she's asking me how I am. She's like, 'I'm fine. This sucks, but I'm going to be fine.' I absolutely believe that. There's nothing she won't do."

Every day at practice was a chance for Gruss to get better for tomorrow, Knights Assistant Athletic Director Diane Karst said. Gruss always made sure she was doing her best so everyone else could get better because of it.

Renier remembers when Gruss was a freshman and no junior varsity player wanted to guard her because they'd get beat up. She was hard-nosed, and she outworked everyone. She still plays the same way, aggressive and a little mean, and hates that her defense isn't as good as it could be.

"I'm not as fast in the chair yet, and I really need to work on my mechanics," she said. "I was always the kid who would go for any ball, so it's a little different when I do it now. I just don't end up on the floor as much."

But she still usually comes up with the ball.

"Watching her play now and seeing the joy in her face does you good to see that none of this is holding her back," Renier said. "That's just Shelby."

The first time Gruss went back onto a basketball court at Turnstone Center in Fort Wayne, she was nervous knowing she'd be weak, and she hates being terrible at anything. She didn't know how to play the game she'd always loved or work the chair or adapt to teammates. The teammates helped her get adjusted, teasing her almost immediately because she was the only girl.

The worst part? Going from being able to make a three-pointer with some regularity to not being able to make a free throw. Gruss always took pride in her form, but she'd had to adjust it to get enough air under her shots, and now her range is decent out to 16 feet.

But maybe she's doing it all wrong. Players who've been in wheelchairs a lot longer never tried to develop perfect form, and they can put the ball in from almost anywhere. She, however, can't adjust what is already ingrained and shakes her head in disgust (and sometimes awe) at how accurate her teammates can be.

Basketball also has provided insight into her new life. If there's something she doesn't know how to do, someone else has already figured it out and is willing to share. She had no idea there was such a large physically challenged population, and now she's got a new culture of friends, teammates and competitors.

But she's still a daredevil. She's already revisited the accident scene, this time to ski. She's learning archery, has become a precocious tennis player and rides horses. With the help of friends, she even took part in a Tough Mudder challenge recently and has plans for another in the fall. The announcer said she was the toughest person he knew.

"It made me realize that absolutely nothing is impossible, especially when you have support and a team. I think a lot of people aren't willing to ask for help sometimes because they have to prove they can do it themselves, and that's me. I want to do anything I can by myself, but there are a lot of things you can do if you just ask for a hand, and a lot of people are willing to help."

It's like Gruss is finding new ways to climb back into her old life. Kuhn said Gruss was the toughest competitor ever to come out of Bishop Luers.

"I think there's a reason for this," Kuhn said. "I don't know what it is, but she's going to change the world, and I've always told her that. I can't imagine anything stopping her, ever."

Gruss is tough, adventurous, and the best way to get her to do something has always been to express doubt about her. She gladly embraces that challenge.

Maybe, someone suggests, God picked her for this as an example.

"It might have been God's plan. I've accepted what's happened, but I think someday I'll be able to walk again. If God wants me to do it, He's going to let me."

Someday soon, Gruss wants a tattoo, probably on her back. She wants the line from the end of the poem "Footprints in the Sand," where a person looks back on their life walking alongside Christ only to see one set of footprints at times.

"I want the last line, 'And that's when I carried you.'"

Gruss also knows that at the end of the poem there are two sets of footprints.

CHAPTER 25
Mom's illness inspires senior season
Published Feb. 24, 2007, in The News-Sentinel

At almost every Canterbury High School basketball game, there would be a guy in the stands getting laughs from his friends by yelling something he thought was witty. He would be trying, begging almost, to get a reaction from basketball star Megan King.

The hecklers probably didn't know King had bigger distractions in her life than they could ever provide. She might have spent the night before in the hospital, praying as her mother fought for life. Or maybe it was spent helping her mother, Jamie, shave her head for the first time. Or maybe she was awake all night, helping her father care for her mother.

Jamie King is fighting cancer, a fight she ultimately can't win. Megan is the state's second-leading scorer, at 27 points per game, and the leader of a No. 3-ranked Canterbury team that completed its season in the regional Feb. 17. But she's been so much more than that this season.

Megan never let anyone see a crack in her shell until after the game. A few times, it was all she could do to run to the locker room, grab her clothes and dash to the parking lot before letting her emotions out. Only her teammates, coaches and family really knew. Everyone else saw only strength, composure and excellence.

"If you didn't know the circumstances, you would have no idea," Canterbury coach Scott Kreiger said. "Everyone gears up to stop her, beat her up or get her off her game. I've even seen coaches yelling at her. She just lets it roll off her back. She has been so good in her approach to the game and her maturity."

It hasn't been a great senior year for Megan. It has been a remarkable one.

RALLYING AROUND MOM

On the morning of Sept. 15, Jamie King noticed a lump on the side of her neck. She called her husband, family doctor Mark King, back into the house to ask about it before he left for work. After some tests, another tumor was discovered on the other side of her neck.

Since then, Jamie has been through surgery and chemotherapy, but the cancer won't give up. Her daughters, former Bishop Luers stars Rachel, 24, and Michelle, 22, have come home, Rachel from her teaching and coaching jobs in Charleston, S.C., and Michelle from her senior year at DePauw University. Mark has taken a leave of absence from his practice.

Everyone came to rally around Mom and each other. That helped Jamie find acceptance and peace, and then everyone else found peace from that.

"I think the best thing that happened, that settled my mind, was when Michelle got engaged and Megan got accepted to the College of Charleston where Rachel is," Jamie said. "Mark is a grown man, and he will go help families here. It was like all this was meant to be. God had a plan for me, but for the girls too, so everybody could be watched and taken care of. I just felt like all of our lives had fallen into place."

The Kings have always been close-knit, but now nothing gets left unsaid, no hug held back. "I've always believed God only gives you what you can handle," Jamie said. "If it's a lot, it's a lot."

They've all prayed and talked things out and believe they are prepared. The girls know they'll be better mothers someday because of what they've learned.

"I don't know why this happened, but I never asked why," Rachel said. "She brought us up with so much faith that we know why. All of the good things that have come out of this are unbelievable. None of us want to see her suffer, but that comes along with her now being at peace with everything and knowing that everyone else is at peace."

FINDING A DISTRACTION

About the only normal thing in the Kings' lives has been watching Megan's senior season. Everyone — grandparents, aunts, uncles and cousins included — have attended the games. For two hours, the games were their distraction. Rachel and Michelle saw it as a blessing to be able to watch their little sister play, something they otherwise would have missed.

The situation could have put more pressure on Megan, who wanted desperately to perform well for her mother, but she adored seeing people who love her sitting in the stands. "Oh, my gosh, is she tough," Rachel said. "She's mature beyond her years, and I think that shows on the basketball court. I remember when she had to shave Mom's head, and she called me and said it was probably the worst thing she's ever had to do in her life, but she did it.

"There was nothing else to do but get through it. Somehow. She couldn't imagine anyone else helping with it."

"It was so hard, and I tried to stay strong enough because we were both crying," Megan said. "Even as a kid, you always remember the smell of your mom's hair. I miss that. Everyone does."

That's how Megan is Jamie's daughter. Jamie is her inspiration and role model. She's showing everything her mother has taught her, proving to Jamie that she's going to be OK, that she will have a great life, a Christian life graced and led by faith.

"She's a wonderful person," Megan said, "and so many don't have the opportunity to become as close as we all are with her. She has shaped us into the people we are. Just to be half the woman she is would be everything. We are so lucky to have someone like that in our lives."

FIGHTING THROUGH

But there have been some brutally difficult games and times, including the recent death of Mark King's mother.

Megan started the season by passing the 2,000-point career mark. During a stop in play, Kreiger handed Megan the ball and she climbed into the stands to give it to Jamie, along with a kiss and a hug. There were few dry eyes in the stands.
"I had no idea she would bring me the ball, but she wanted to share it with me," Jamie said. "I'm like, don't bring this attention to me, this is for you to go out there and jump up and down. I want to be there for every game because it's so moving."

There have been a few games Jamie has had to miss, including against Harding, which Megan knew would be difficult. Because Megan's AAU teammate and friend Rashida Ray plays for Harding, and because Jamie knows so many Harding parents, Megan knew she'd have to explain the situation before the game. "I think she was there helping me get through that really hard mental time. Somehow, I pulled it through, and I don't know how that happened."

"Pulled it through" meant scoring 37 points as the Cavaliers won perhaps their biggest game of the season. After the game, Megan sobbed as Rachel drove home.

LEANING ON TEAMMATES

Whenever Megan has lost control, her teammates have been there. Knowing Jamie could not come to New Haven one night, Megan told teammate Stacia Gerardot before the game she needed help and that she didn't know how much she could give. Gerardot responded by scoring 21 points to become the first Cavalier other than King to lead the team in scoring during the last four seasons.

A week after the New Haven game, captains Gerardot and Aubrey Holle presented Megan with blue and white armbands with the initials JK on them. Everyone on the team wore the bands.

On Senior Night, the Gerardot sisters gave Megan a card telling her what an inspiration she is.

"Their faith is just unbelievable, and I look up to them so much because of it," Megan said. "My teammates have been wonderful and have meant so much to me."

FINDING INSPIRATION

Many in the Canterbury community have been inspired by Jamie and Megan's experiences. It seems everyone has learned something from this. Everyone has been changed.

"It's just amazing how many people have been touched by the experience that (the Kings) are going through, and touched in a positive way," coach Kreiger said. "I'm sure there are things that are not left unsaid among families or even among kids because of this."

Megan's relationship with Kreiger's son, Colten, has allowed her to continue laughing and have someplace to go when she needs to get away and relax.

"I pray about things a lot," she said. "Your faith will always make you better. God obviously has this plan for my mom, and he's trying to teach us to get through this. We can't hate him for it."

Before every game, Megan asked God to let her do her best so she could make her mom proud. It was never in doubt.

"All she ever wants to know is, 'Did I play good enough?'" Jamie said. "It's like she never feels like she gave 100 percent. What more can you do out there? Look at your knees, your legs, your body. You've done it all and helped everybody else. What more could you do?"

SENIOR PRIDE

So, no, Megan King never pays attention to the hecklers in the stands. Her sisters marvel at how she keeps her cool, knowing that each of them would have struggled, but Megan said she has learned so many important things this year.

"It's times like these that you realize who cares and who doesn't," she said. "It's hard because not everyone deals with this kind of thing the same way.

"You realize that some people don't care as much, and that's one of the biggest, shocking things. You have to take everyone for who they are, and you have to accept everyone and not find fault in their weaknesses.

"I've been very blessed to have people surround me who understand. Some things, you can't overcome mentally, but I am so lucky to be blessed with such good friends."

It hasn't been the greatest senior year, but it's still one she can be proud of — just as her mother could not be more proud of her daughter.

CHAPTER 26
Rich in faith, Bonivenger Misiko leaves his future to God
Published June 23, 2005, in The News-Sentinel

Would you have this kind of faith in yourself and your God?

The Fort Wayne Fever's Bonivenger Misiko got the phone call to leave Nairobi, Kenya, and come to America three years ago. Because the second semester was already starting at Lindsey Wilson College in Columbia, Ky., he needed to get there as quickly as possible. There wasn't even time to wait for his mother to return from his grandmother's funeral to say goodbye. Some friends advised him to wait and take the next opportunity, but others said that might never come.

He left with about 12 items of clothing, leaving more behind for a younger brother. He had nothing else except the dream of playing soccer at Lindsey Wilson, a school recommended by a friend of Lindsey coach Ray Wells.

"You meet thousands of people there like Bonny who have

nothing in terms of material wealth, but they have hope and a vision of what they want their life to be sometime in the future," said Wells, who has made five trips to Kenya. "They don't squander opportunities."

On the first leg of the plane ride, another man from Kenya gave Misiko $10, which he used after traveling more than a day to eat his first American food when he arrived in Louisville, Ky.

"It was so cold," he said. "Inside the airport is still warm, but once they opened the doors, I was so cold."

He had never seen snow, knew no one or anything about the school, and had never even talked with Wells. He had used English in schools, but it was mostly to read and it wasn't like this, where everyone talked so fast. Besides the weather, the thing that surprised him the most was the paved roads.

"My mom used to pray that, 'One day, my kids are going to lift me up,'" Misiko said. "I see this as God giving my mom a blessing in me coming here and, God willing, (graduating) so I can get a good job and help my family."

Would you have that kind of faith in yourself and your God?

The school set him up with a host family, and Misiko, 24, started learning the culture and working on the language. With little or no money, he focuses on his studies. An outstanding student, he's an accounting major because he figures it will be a marketable skill at home. Sometimes he calls home, but he communicates mostly through e-mail. Misiko loves movies and playing for the Fever, whom he played for last year. He said he has no idea what he'd be doing if he hadn't come back this year. The team is allowed to supply him with an apartment but can't do much else because of NAIA rules. He's prohibited from working because he's here on a student visa. Sometimes, teammates will pick up his tab for a meal or movie.

"He's definitely content with who he is, where he is in life and where he wants to go," said the Fever's Drew Shinabarger. "You have to respect what he's doing, especially when you have so many kids who are so spoiled. You just try to help him out where you can."

It's going to be a while before Misiko returns home, because he'd rather send any money he receives back than spend it on a plane ticket. His parents, three brothers and a sister live in one of the poorest parts of Africa.

"What happens in Kenya, if you come here, they think you are going to get money," he said. "Most people think their problems are solved, but I can't work."

Fortunately, friends will buy him the necessities his scholarship doesn't cover, such as deodorant. Other times, a Canadian family friend will send money, and Fever fans have been known to make donations of food and clothing.

"The funny thing is, I lack for nothing," he says.

Nothing?

"I pray," he said. "I believe in God. That's all I need."

His visa is set to expire in December. How will he get around that to earn the money to send home?

"I believe in God and that everything is going to work out

eventually," he said. "God will provide."

Would you have this kind of faith in yourself and your God?

CHAPTER 27
Faith gives Keion Henderson strength in comeback
Published Feb. 28, 2004, in The News-Sentinel

After Keion Henderson's knee buckled and he crumpled to the court on Jan. 31, 2002, the IPFW forward figured God was trying to get his attention. A torn anterior cruciate ligament meant his junior collegiate season was over, and Henderson was wondering if God was trying to tell him to forget basketball and get on with his calling as a Baptist minister.

Henderson now believes God was trying to get his attention in a different way.

"I thought this was just me being a hardhead trying to ignore it," Henderson said. "Now I look back, and I don't think that's what was going on."

Following a family tradition, Henderson became a minister at an early age. His father and two brothers were already preaching, but little brother was determined to be different.

"I was at school with my pants hanging off and my hat turned toward the side trying to have my own identity," he said. "I found out very quickly that that wasn't me."

One day when he was 14, Henderson was sitting in his father's Gary, Ind., church when he started to cry. He felt the message was being directed to him.

"I asked God if this is what he wanted me to do, because I was too afraid to even go up there in front of the church," he said.

As if by divine direction, at that moment, a pastor friend approached from behind and whispered in Henderson's ear, "I see you're dealing with some things," the man said. "If you need somebody to walk up with you, I will."

That gave Henderson the strength to get up and start his new life. Seven days later, he presented his first sermon in front of 900 people.

"I had to use the bathroom about four times before the service," he said, laughing.

Continuing to preach, Henderson eventually became an ordained minister.

The knee injury and the year off gave him time to concentrate on his ministry, but he didn't give up on basketball. He kept up with his rehabilitation and fought his way back onto the court.

"He's just one of the most remarkable young men I've ever been around," IPFW coach Doug Noll said. "He's so grounded and understands at a young age what he needs to do. He's going take all these life lessons he's learned through basketball and make himself a better pastor."

Part of that adversity has been IPFW's 3-23 record. There's also been finding the time and strength to complete his church work. While his teammates are goofing around on bus rides or plane flights, Henderson is writing his sermons and listening to inspirational tapes. While they are sleeping, he's often talking to congregation members needing help.

"I don't think a normal student could handle everything that he has," Noll said. "He's doing some important things with his life already."

Through this long season, Henderson eventually figured out that the adversity was God's true message from his knee injury. Being a pastor, he said, isn't all about wins, but how you react to the losses.

"I've learned a lot from this year to help me out in my life," he said. "I know now, even though the injury was the most painful thing I've ever been through, it had a purpose as far as being able to be mentally tough and pushing through and being able to take a lot of things at one time. I know it's a direct result of my injury, because I wasn't as mentally tough before."

As his career winds down this week, he's been playing his best basketball. Over his last three games, Henderson has averaged 19 points. He's making the best of his final games.

"This year has meant an opportunity for me to finish what I started," Henderson said. "It was meant for me to realize that no matter how tough the obstacle is, giving up is not an option. If losing basketball games is the most difficult thing I ever have to go through, then I've had a good life. Basketball is significant and I love it, but preaching is my passion. That's what I'll do for the rest of my life."

CHAPTER 28
Prayer sustained Komet and his wife during off-ice challenge
Published June 21, 2006, in The News-Sentinel

Guy and Nicole Dupuis believe sometimes God reaches down to tap them on the shoulder.

Sometimes it's to remind them of something. Other times it's to get their attention, and once in a while, it's just to let them know God is there.

They've had quite a few taps lately, and luckily, they've known exactly what each one meant. The Komets defenseman and his wife used their faith to provide stability and strength during a very trying challenge late in the season.

When Nicole was six months pregnant with their third child, she started carrying extra amniotic fluid and having preterm labor problems. On Feb. 7, their doctor reported several troubling areas in the ultra-sound test and wanted the couple to see another doctor.

The second doctor agreed the child had several abnormalities and said he was 70 percent sure the baby had trisomy 18, which affects one of every 3,000 births, or trisomy 13, which occurs in one of every 5,000 births. In either case, life-sustaining measures are not recommended before birth. The couple was told the baby likely would not live to be born or would not live for very long thereafter.

"The baby was in a breech position, and the doctor explained that a normal delivery would result in his death," Nicole said. "The doctor said he wouldn't recommend a Cesarean section because the baby would likely die at or shortly after birth."

Further tests were ordered.

"He tells us there's a 70 percent chance that the baby is not going to survive a few days, a week or two months, and a 30 percent chance he might make it two or three years," Guy said. "He did not think this was a child with Down syndrome."

Devastated, Guy and Nicole went home to begin mourning the death of their son, to pray and prepare their children, Brooke, 9, and Mitchell, 7. The four decided to name the baby Matthew, meaning "Gift of the Lord." Their priest, Father John Kuzmich at St. Vincent's Catholic Church, met with them to pray.

After Guy and Nicole told a few family members and friends, a prayer chain started that grew to include hundreds, and then thousands, of people. A call from a friend in Bakersfield, Calif., where Guy had played in 2002-03, said there were more than 600 people praying for them.

"What was comforting for us and helped us through was taking the attitude that life is a gift, and if God gives us an opportunity to have Matthew for a few hours, weeks or months, we were going to cherish that gift," Guy said.

"That helped us to be positive and more optimistic. It was out of our control and in His, and that helped us. We're (Matthew's) parents, and if something happens and we don't get to meet him here, then we'll get to be his parents one day in heaven."

When Nicole experienced signs of preterm labor, she called her doctor and told him she wanted something to stop the labor at least until further tests came back.

"I just couldn't live with thinking that delivering this child was going to kill him since he was breech," she said.

Four days later, the report came back saying the original diagnosis was wrong. The problem was trisomy 21, or Down syndrome. The doctor was baffled and asked how aggressively Nicole wanted to be treated.

"Whatever I have to do, I'll do to keep the baby in there," she said.

Meanwhile, the family continued to pray, as did thousands in expanding prayer chains.

Nicole would lie in bed each morning praying over the baby. Some people congratulated the couple on having a Down syndrome baby.

"People we would talk to were like, 'I'm sorry and I hope this doesn't offend you, congratulations,'" Nicole said.

"Whoever gets congratulated that their kid has Down syndrome? For me that was great. I wonder if it happened that way so that we'd be excited for Matthew to come into our family."

There were other moments when they felt God's tapping. Guy had left Fort Wayne and the Komets in 1999 but came back this year when his family needed to be at home with Nicole's parents, friends and their church. Nicole's parents live next to family friends Jenny and Joe Bockerstette — who have a daughter with Down syndrome and co-founded the Down Syndrome Association of Northeast Indiana.

"We already had a group of people in place to both educate and support us," Nicole said.

When Nicole was 28 weeks into her pregnancy, because of the extra amniotic fluid, she measured as if she were 38 weeks along. The doctor checked her weekly to see if she needed some fluid drained. The procedure carries a chance of infection or miscarriage, however.

"We kept asking people for prayers, and they kept asking other people," Nicole said. "I got a card from a lady I don't know who had a child with trisomy 18 that died a couple of months after birth. She just wanted to let me know that she and her husband were praying for Matthew. I was so touched that they knew his name, let alone were praying for us every night."

"Honestly, the way that our friends and family prayed for us and asked others for prayers was amazing.

"We certainly didn't feel alone going through this."

During this entire time, Guy continued to go to practice and play defense for the Komets. He missed one practice and one road game. His teammates supported him, and a couple said they were praying for him.

When he was at the games, he gave his cell phone to Komets trainer Shawn Dundon in case Nicole called in an emergency, because she was still experiencing signs of preterm labor. A couple of times, he was within a few seconds of going onto the ice when he'd call Nicole to see whether or not he should play.

"It affected me emotionally somewhat," Guy said. "You have your normal mindset before you go to the game, but I'd be home being wrapped up in all of this. It was difficult, but it also gave me a little time to focus just on hockey and have a release. I wasn't able to do that every game. It takes a toll on you."

After playing exceptionally well in February, his statistics slipped down the stretch, but Dupuis was still named the Komets' best defenseman. The Komets ended their regular season April 15. The next day — on Easter — Matthew was born.

"We both burst into tears because he was six weeks early," Nicole said. "We knew that with Down syndrome, he could have a lot of complications anyway, but coming this early, we knew he could be in a lot of trouble."

It was determined an emergency Cesarean section was necessary, and Matthew was born 18 inches long and weighing 5 pounds, 14 ounces.

While Matthew stayed in intensive care for 12 days, his father would go to practice and then sleep at the hospital.

Finally, Matthew got to go home, where Guy's mother had arrived from Canada to pitch in along with Nicole's parents. The family kept asking for more prayers.

"I honestly believe it's the prayers that have made him as healthy as he is," Nicole said. "He's real strong. He has already rolled over at six weeks. From here, we just love him and take care of him like we do our other kids."

Several weeks later, as Nicole holds Matthew in her lap to feed him, a heart monitor's lights flash from the floor. Everywhere Matthew goes, the monitor gets picked up and goes with him. He's been quarantined for a few weeks to protect him from infections but has consistently gained weight.

One of the Dupuis' friends said that if ever there was a perfect family for such a baby to be born into, this is it. God has given him to a family that can handle the problems.

"Let's see what the future holds for him," Guy said. "Right now, we are focusing on the blessing that he is in our lives. He really is a gift from God."

As he sleeps in his mother's lap, Matthew has no idea he has already affected thousands of people.

"He's been pretty blessed, and he doesn't even know it," Nicole said. "We don't feel like God is done working miracles with him."

CHAPTER 29
DaMarcus Beasley's leap of faith
Published June 14, 2014, in The News-Sentinel

Ever since DaMarcus Beasley started playing soccer, even against older players, he loved using his speed, strength and creativity to attack. As one of the Americans' most consistent scoring threats for 10 years, he was always pushing defenders back as they tried anticipating where his dancing sprint might charge next.

But then the United States needed somebody to stop those threats. After a particularly tough loss in March 2013, men's national team coach Jurgen Klinsmann called Beasley to ask what he thought about switching from midfield to left back. It was a risky, gutsy move for Klinsmann, and an even bigger gamble for Beasley.

"I still had lots to accomplish with the national team, and I didn't feel like my time was over yet," Beasley said. "I said of course. We're professionals, and we want to be on the field at any time."

Except it wasn't that simple or easy. Imagine Joey Votto changing from first base to shortstop or Andrew Luck moving from quarterback to safety. Think how hard it would be to think about the game in a completely different way, and oh, try to do it at the World Cup competition level. Imagine changing a lifetime of habits.

That's a lot to ask of a 32-year-old, because nobody hates change more than elite athletes, who are slaves to their routines. Also, this wasn't a "just give it a shot" thing as much as an unspoken "make this work or you're probably off the team."

"He told me he would play whatever role we asked, and he has proven his point over the last several months with some tremendous performances," Klinsmann told USSoccer.com. "He's a great guy to have around the locker room. He always has a smile on his face and brings a lot of positive energy."

At least publicly — and, he says, personally — Beasley never blinked, never doubted, never questioned. He didn't have time to; learning the new position needed to be done quickly. He also had to set the example for the rest of his younger teammates, who were wondering if he could do it.

It was almost a decision to prove he was just as good as his confidence showed. Second-guessing would take too much time.

The goal, as Beasley said, was now to stop strikers from doing to him what he'd been trying to do to others for so long.

Maybe the biggest advantage he had was that he knew how he would attack midfielders, so now he had to take away scoring opportunities instead of creating them. Despite not being the biggest or strongest midfielder, he might be the quickest with the best ability to recover.

"He's so versatile that even though he's been playing as a wide midfielder or a wide forward, he possesses the most important essential," said Fort Wayne United coach and longtime friend Bobby Pousanidis. "He has an incredible ability to think quickly and apply that to his decision-making skills. I used to think he could excel at this position because he is so quick and so hard to get around, but he can also get the ball up the field. It adds an extra weapon that a team may need."

It's an odd combination of confidence and humility that allows Beasley to make this switch in a World Cup year. He's confident enough in his ability to know he has the physical and thinking skills to make it work, and he has the humility to accept the change quickly as being best for the team. He's got to believe in himself and the move, which may not be the same things.

This had to come down to faith, and not necessarily just faith in himself. Beasley had to believe this was God's intended role for him. He and God had been through a lot with soccer, from moving around the world trying to find spots to play and a team to fit in on, to reacting to racist attacks. There had to be inner strength, because often there was no one else there with him.

"I told him every time there was a door closing, 'But God opened another door, and it's always bigger than the door that's closing in your face,'" Beasley's father, Henry, said. "This is a faith thing as well, and as long as he keeps believing and doing what he's supposed to, he's going to be fine."

OK, it's one thing for Mom or Dad to talk about God and faith and what if and how come. After all, they are supposed to set that standard and have more life experience to use as examples, but sometimes living through those moments isn't nearly as clear. It's sometimes hard to see God's plan when you are the one He's manipulating.

"It really was a big part of this," DaMarcus said. "Even if I thought things were not going the way they were supposed to go, I have always had faith that God would open that next door for me to walk through. A lot of what I do is based on the grounding I have with faith."

And maybe that's the real reason Beasley is still around to play in his fourth World Cup. He's gone from being the next future star, to then trying to fulfill potential, to now becoming a team leader and a key example. Maybe he needed to go through everything else to get to the point that might become the height of his career.

Maybe instead of taking chances with the ball all the time, he had to learn to take a chance on himself and trust his coach's decision. Maybe it is all about faith, just in a different way than we normally expect from athletes.

"My dad's line has always been in my head ever since I started playing," Beasley said. "Whenever I've had bad times or a bad game, he always kept me positive with that. Now, I still have confidence I can still play at this level. God never gives you more than you can handle."

CHAPTER 30
Rod Woodson found peace when he answered God's call
Published Dec. 31, 1999, in The News-Sentinel

There have been many points when Rod Woodson's athletic future could have been altered.

* As a youngster, the only reason he started playing organized football was because his brothers pushed him into the Police Athletic League program. He liked football but didn't love it until much later. Coach Dave Rody positioned Woodson as a defensive back because "he had great ability to see what was going on. He was our golden parachute — if you can get past everything, you're not going to get past the kid with the wheels at the end."

* As a Snider High School sophomore, Woodson quit the junior varsity football squad for several games only to be talked into going back to it by his track coach, Jim Gurnell. Woodson didn't care for coaches yelling at him all the time.

"I believed that (if) you're not my parents, I don't need you yelling and screaming at me. If you want me to do something, just tell me. That's the kind of attitude I had."

* As a junior, Woodson only played tailback after senior John Ramsey went down with a knee injury during the state playoffs. Woodson had been a slotback, but Ramsey was a Division I-caliber running back. Woodson soon proved he was, too.

Woodson finished with 576 yards on 100 carries. During his senior year, he carried 77 times for 758 yards and 12 touchdowns.

"We didn't know he was going to be an NFL player, but we knew pretty quickly he was going to be a Division I great one," Snider coach Mike Hawley said.

* Woodson chose Purdue University over the University of Michigan and several other football factories because he thought he wanted to become an electrical engineer. After realizing he couldn't study engineering and play football, Woodson finished with a criminal justice degree.

He also finished as one of Purdue's all-time greats.

In perhaps the best individual performance in a Purdue game, on Nov. 22, 1986, Woodson was a one-man wrecking crew against Indiana University. From his normal position as a defensive back, he had 10 tackles, forced a fumble to set up a touchdown and broke up a pass. Playing for the first time in his college career on offense, Woodson ran 15 times for 93 yards and caught three passes for 67 yards.

* After his senior season at Purdue, Woodson went to California in 1987 to study how to run the hurdles and then to Europe to compete in track during the NFL players' strike. Though he was a Big Ten indoor champion and an All-American, he had never worked much on his technique at a high level. If the strike hadn't ended …

"Maybe in retrospect, if I had to do it over again, I probably would have stayed out and run track for the year," he said. "I was enjoying it that much. As (an) amateur in track, I could not have professional status in one sport and get my amateur status in another at that time. You can now. I wish we could have then, because I'd have done both."

Instead, he came home, joined the NFL and will complete his 13th season Sunday, his second with the Baltimore Ravens. His career includes being named to the NFL's 75th anniversary team in 1994 and the NFL's 30th-best player of all time by Pro Football Weekly in January 1997. He has tied the NFL career record for interception returns for touchdown with nine and is tied with Willie Brown for 16th on the all-time interception list with 54.

Woodson had seven interceptions through 15 games this season with Baltimore and was named to the Pro Bowl for the eighth time. He made history, becoming the first Pro Bowler at cornerback, safety and kick returner.

As he looks back now at age 34, Woodson doesn't like to focus too long on what might have happened in his life. All he knows is that a lot of things went the right way.

"Everything happens for a reason, and I've been blessed," Woodson said. "There's no reason to second-guess it. God has blessed me with wonderful talent throughout my life, a wonderful family, a great foundation and great coaches. He gave me a beautiful wife and four beautiful kids. If I complain, I need to be skinned alive, because I've had it all.

"There's nothing about it I wouldn't do over again. All the decisions I've made in my life, all the mistakes I've made, all the right decisions I've made, have been a part of my growth. You live and learn. It takes you a while."

Woodson said it took him several years to accept that knowledge and peace, several years of always searching for more. Getting married and fathering his first child changed his perspective some. He sees this process as God's way of giving him a wake-up call.

"At that point, God was ringing the phone, but I wasn't answering it then," Woodson said. "I was still doing my own thing, being Rod Woodson. A year ago, I answered the phone, and I've been blessed. I'm still a baby in Christ. I've been on and off the path my whole life. It's better being on the path than off it."

In what ways?

"You definitely have to be more humble," he said. "I was a humble person anyway, I believe, but that made me more humble, less proud about things. I was always a laid-back, easygoing person. I've always been on an even keel. Being with Christ, I'm at peace with everything right now. Every decision I make now I know has a reason because He is leading me that way. I know in the future he'll put his hand on me and guide me in the right way. He'll take me into what he wants me to do."

Right now, Woodson believes, God wants him to keep playing football and return to Fort Wayne each summer to continue his football camp for area youth. He knows every kid on the Snider High School field wants to follow him to the NFL. He doesn't discourage that hope, but he does try to temper it.

"The one statement I make is that wisdom is so much stronger than strength on any given day of life," Woodson said. "Even if you do play sports, especially in football, the great players understand the sport, and the reason they understand it is they study the game."

Which is what he does so well now. This year, the Ravens

moved Woodson from cornerback to safety, but he spent most of his time working to teach the new cornerback. The only personal goal he has left is to get a championship ring. He knows time is running out, but it's not gone yet.

"I've never made a timetable," he said. "When I came into the league, John Stallworth, Mike Webster, Donnie Shell and those guys were still playing and Chuck Noll was my coach. Donnie said, 'I played for 12 years,' and I'm thinking, '12 years? I can't play for 12 years.' Even after Year 5, I was thinking that's seven more years, and that won't happen. Now I'm eight years into it, and I still love it."

CHAPTER 31
Coach battling cancer with positive energy
Published Feb. 10, 2016, in The News-Sentinel

On the night of his 21st birthday, the car Kevin Kraner was riding in veered off the road into a massive wreck. He broke an arm and leg, shattered his jaw and suffered severe head trauma — and he was declared dead on arrival. As part of a near-death experience, he saw his mother and brother looking on in the operating room and then experienced a light at the end of a long tunnel before hearing voices say, "Everything is all going to be OK." He woke up in the recovery room days later.

He survived death once and always wondered why.

* * *

Kraner, now 40, has always been a little bit stubborn when dealing with medical issues. He was brought up in Ligonier, Ind., to be independent, self-disciplined and a fighter, which helped during his rehabilitation, especially after being told he'd likely never walk without a limp or regain full function in his arm. Kraner said he wouldn't be back to therapy until he decided he couldn't do it alone.

Teaching himself, the process took three years. Along the way, he went to Vincennes University for a year before transferring to Purdue University, where he studied exercise science and made the Purdue football practice squad as a walk-on. Graduating in 2001, he started working through Orthopaedics NorthEast at IPFW with the men's and women's basketball and women's volleyball teams before moving around to Spiece Fitness, Anytime Fitness, Personal Training Institute and Parkview Hospital. Two years ago, he started at Empowered Sports Club as assistant general manager in charge of strength and conditioning, membership and fitness. A big part of his focus is the volleyball program.

He had always used the things he'd learned during his car crash rehab in his professional life, especially emphasizing that strength and conditioning include the mind as much as the body.

Then this October, he started suffering back pain. As someone who lives in a weight room, at first, he figured he'd lifted something incorrectly.

"It would come and go, but it was never a consistent thing," he said. "One day, I could hardly walk because my back hurt and I couldn't make any sudden moves or turns, and the next day, I would be golden and I'm running and doing everything I do in the gym."

But the pain increased in November and December, and Kraner

was told it was likely a kidney stone. In the early morning of Dec. 19, Kraner woke his wife Lindsey to ask her to take him to the emergency room. After more pain medication, he felt better and was sent home. That afternoon, he was doing some shopping when the pain returned, and it took him about 45 minutes of small steps to walk back to his car. The pain dropped him to his knees several times. That night, he went back to the ER and requested additional testing.

"I was expecting something with a disk, herniation, who knows? Maybe surgery or a cortisone shot," he said.

An MRI found two masses wrapped around and through his spine, and two biopsies found the cancer had spread to his spleen, abdomen and groin area, moving him into Stage 4 of a type of non-Hodgkin's lymphoma. After three days of radiation treatment and a week at home to continue praying and regrouping, Kraner started chemotherapy. For the next five months, he'll do five days of treatment followed by two weeks off. The body he had built up over two decades as his tool in his livelihood was now attacking him.

"The doctors told me I've been preparing my whole life for this," he said. "Only God knows why that's true. When it comes to the spiritual aspects, only God knows the path you are going to travel, but maybe I've been preparing my body for this that whole time."

The Kraners' faith, family, co-workers and friends have sustained them. A group of friends started a GoFundMe drive and have raised almost $22,000. A group of about 25 gathered around Kevin's hospital bed to celebrate Christmas Eve with a small candlelight service, and he's spent time studying the Bible and talking about faith with Lindsey and others.

"He's very regimented and always likes to have a plan," Lindsey said. "Now his plan has changed a little bit. He's not going to be able to work out and train every day, but he's still feeding himself mentally. He's focusing on having those people around him who will feed his knowledge to help him through it."

The support has been amazing, from the Empowered Volleyball Academy players forming his name on the court for a picture, to countless hugs, endless prayers from friends and notes from former clients. They have all strengthened Kraner. He can wrap his arms around a crowd of people who love him and then reach even further for more and never run out.

As a strength coach, his goal has always been to make his clients stronger, faster and more confident, enabling them to do things they never thought they could. He taught them to believe that he could help them improve, and now they are the ones telling him to have faith.

"I was never physically strong until I was mentally strong to get myself to that point," he said. "It took me a while in the hospital and lots of talks with my wife to get myself mentally ready for this, to understand that the next few months are going to be pure hell, worse than anything I've ever gone through. In the end, I'm going to have to be the one who is standing tall because I'll have to be mentally strong to get through this.

"If I get defeated mentally, I'm going to get defeated physically. Everyone is telling me, 'You need to believe you can get better,' and I do."

But if he thinks about getting through the whole process, all those months of treatment, the task can be overwhelming and daunting. Instead, the Kraners are focused on one day at a time, something Kevin's used to as a coach, embracing the challenge instead of being intimidated by it.

"It's a path I've never traveled, a path of the unknown, so each day you have to get up and know that day is the first and last you may have, so you have to be strong with it. I don't know what's going to be thrown my way. Of course, I'm scared because of the unknown, but now I'm like, 'Bring it on, let's get through it!' I just have to go with it and be headstrong and go right at it."

In other words, he'll attack it like a coach preparing his team, always doing one more, showing no fear and picturing success before the attempt. This is what he has to do and how he has to do it, and his faith will help him. That may sound like a simple platitude, but the Kraners deeply believe it's truth. The spiritual side of this will be even more important than the physical, they believe.

"We know that God knew this was going to happen a long time ago," Lindsey said. "It's just what it is, and it's really neat to see the people God provides to help us through this. I have faith that God's plan is going to be what it is, and we'll do our best to go through it and have a story at the end."

Did Kraner survive the car accident so that he would be better prepared to take on this challenge?

"I haven't thought about that, but I would say I wasn't as faithful as I am now, and I learned a lot from that," he said. "I cheated death once and I was lucky. Apparently, I was left here for a reason, and I'd say this experience has definitely humbled me a lot and forced me to take a step back.

"I've got to be strong, trust in God, the physicians, the nurses and the whole process. I can't give myself any kind of doubt. If I get defeated mentally, I'll get defeated physically. I have to keep remembering, 'I can do anything through Christ who strengthens me.'"

UPDATE: Two years later, Kraner is doing well, and regular three-month scans have shown he's cancer-free.

CHAPTER 32
Nathanael Moord doesn't let disease run his life
Published Oct. 14, 2003, in The News-Sentinel

As his New Haven Middle School cross country runners were scampering up hills at Central Lutheran School a few weeks ago, coach Bob Walda noticed several of his more talented runners were lollygagging.

"There's something you all need to know and understand," Walda said after gathering his team. "It's important for you as a person to come out and give 100 percent and your very best so when you walk away, you can feel good about that."

Then Walda told his team that one of their teammates had been afflicted with muscular dystrophy, but that same runner was one of the squad's hardest workers.

"Some of you may not know what that means, but it attacks the muscles in the body, and where it's attacking his muscles is in the legs and the hands," Walda said. "His attitude at practice is giving everything that he has to potentially help make himself better. To me, if you could all have that kind of attitude when you are running your hills and in your workouts, how much better would we be as a team?"

A few minutes later as the team was running toward the school, one of the Bulldogs turned to Nathanael "Homey" Moord and asked who he thought the runner was.

"It's me," Nathanael said.

"Aw, c'mon, get real."

"No, it's me, look at my hands."

"I'm so sorry, so sorry."

But actually, Nathanael was fine with it, and the conversation made him feel good about himself. No one suspected, and Walda showed confidence with the talk, all of which meant he was handling things just fine.

Nathanael, 12 years old and a seventh-grader, found out last spring he had the disease. His brother, Josh, 27, found out he had the disease at approximately the same age, and his grandfather also had the disease.

Nathanael had always been one of the top runners in his class during elementary school, but last year, he struggled from the beginning, growing increasingly disappointed when runners he regularly beat before started pulling away.

"There's no frustration now, but there used to be," Nathanael said. "I just wasn't running as fast as I was when I was younger."

His mother, Debbie Moord, started noticing the same symptoms that had affected Josh. The muscles in Nathanael's thumbs started to weaken, and sometimes he'd trip because his foot was dropping.

"When he starts tripping, you kind of know," his mother said. "He tries to laugh and roll and be silly with it, but you know."

When the diagnosis came, at least then he knew what was wrong. That was something he could deal with, and his family could deal with it too.

"The only advice I can give him is to continue to live his life for Jesus Christ," Josh Moord said. "I have one verse that I refer back to, Philippians 4:13: 'I can do all things through Him (who) strengthens me.'

"I think he'll be fine. It won't slow him down at all. Nathanael is a good people-person, and it doesn't matter what disability you have if you are good with people."

So far, he has been very strong, setting personal records three times this season. Currently, his best is 15 minutes, 44 seconds over a 1.9-mile course, and he's shooting for a time in the low 15s before the season ends.

"If somebody asked him about it, he'll talk about it and let you know," teammate Tyler Clark said. "It's not like he slumps around and is all mad about it."

No one knows how long Nathanael will be able to run. Dr. Jerry Mackel, an orthopedic surgeon who has examined Nathanael, said physical activity can't retard the disease but it can retard the effects. He encourages Nathanael to continue competing.

Watching a meet, no one would pick Nathanael out from the pack because of the disease — except possibly for his goofy red and white knee bands — because his stride is smooth, though he regularly finishes near the back.

"I just like to run," he said. "I like all my friends, and I like the running. I still think I can do better. Everybody motivates me and gives me a lot of confidence."

Nathanael's situation and how he has dealt with it has also motivated his teammates.

"The kids don't talk about it a lot, but they have worked much harder since then," Walda said. "Every time he walks away from a meet, every time he walks away from a practice, I think he feels good about it. I think he feels refreshed like he's accomplished something, and I think we all need that."

UPDATE (2018): Nathanael Moord continues to take chances in his life and trust God's path for him. After becoming an English teacher at North Side High School, he has recently decided to explore a career in social work.
"I have just realized that God is going to take care of me and put me in a position He wants me to be in," he said. "He has called me to live a life of joy, and I need to pursue what I feel God is calling me to. If it doesn't fit exactly what I'm looking for, I'm willing to give up some of the money or some of the comforts to do something I am passionate about. Life is short, and I'd rather spend my time doing things that I love doing and impacting people I want to impact and just trust that everything will work out."

CHAPTER 33
Friends keep running to overcome challenges
Published May 5, 2005, in The News-Sentinel

Every once in a while, Brady Long wonders what it's like to be his friend Jon Sharpe, so he'll try closing his eyes just to get a taste of the sensation.

But as the darkness closes in, Long can keep his eyelids clenched for only about 10 seconds before he gets too uncomfortable and has to open them.

"Sometimes you wake up in the middle of the night and have to go to the bathroom (in the dark), and that's about what he can see," he said.

When Long was born 46 years ago, his mother's St. Joseph Hospital room was across the hall from Nancy Sharpe, who had delivered Jon two days earlier. During the first grade at St. Jude Catholic School, the boys became fast friends, playing every sport under the sun together and often not coming home until well past when it had gone down.

When Jon was 10, he was hit in the right eye with a rock and suffered profound vision loss. It didn't slow him down from playing anything he wanted with Brady. In fact, he was the better athlete of the pair.

But when he was 15, a brain tumor took the sight from Sharpe's left eye.

"I remember sitting in class crying because it was devastating," Long said. "He was my brother. That changed my world, too."

Long became determined to make sure blindness would change Sharpe's world as little as possible.

"I remember Brady coming in and saying, 'You're gonna do everything like I do, still; (it's) going to be just like it always was. As far as I'm concerned, things are the same,'" Sharpe said. "He's not going to let you sit there, especially when he knows you want to be up doing something. Brady pushes me to do all kinds of things I wouldn't have done otherwise."

So Long has worked with Sharpe to teach him how to skate, water-ski, shoot baskets and even pass a hockey puck. When they were 16, Long taught Sharpe how to drive around a parking lot, and he's also had him drive a speedboat. This winter, they went with Long's father, former Komet Eddie Long, to skate a 10-mile canal in Ottawa. Someday, they'll work some more on golf.

"He's always saying, 'C'mon, you can do it,'" Sharpe said. "It's never been anything that has endangered my life — as far as I knew, anyway."

To them, it's not an extraordinary story. They figure they'd be doing all of this anyway if Sharpe hadn't had the tumor. Sharpe says he never quit participating in sports — Long just helped him find different ways to play.

"I know it sounds kind of corny, but it would be a big deal if I couldn't do these things," Sharpe said. "These kind of things fill up my life. It would be pretty empty if I didn't have them. These are the memories you can use when you are feeling down and out to just sit there and feel good."

Thirty-one years later, they are still competing side by side.

As they do most years, they'll run in the 500 Festival Mini-Marathon in Indianapolis this weekend. Long will take a three-foot terry cloth rope, wrap it around his left hand and then hand it to Sharpe, who wraps the other end around his right hand. Because Sharpe is three inches taller, he sometimes has to alter his stride a hair. Sharpe likes to run in spurts.

"He's faster than me, but he doesn't have a choice," Long jokes. "He's just going, and I kind of let him lead and let him know where the cracks are or when we need to make a left turn and such."

One year, they finished the Indy race in 2 hours,18.13 seconds, though they've gone as long as 2:45 depending on their training and the weather. This will be the third year they have raised money for Youth for Christ through pledges.

"I really think our getting a pace isn't even a sighted thing, it's a feel thing," Sharpe said. "I almost know when he's going to say when things are feeling pretty good. I think he knows when I'm comfortable, and I know when he's comfortable. We'll just hit that stride, and it feels like we could run forever."

Last year, Joe Doust joined them for the race and, at about eight miles in, offered to carry the tether.

"I just was figuring I could pitch in," he said. "I think I got a mile, and Brady was lagging behind us. He just didn't feel normal without holding onto the tether. He couldn't do anything but grab that thing from my hand, and then he got a big smile on his face, and we were off and going."

"I felt like I couldn't even stay in the race," Long said. "We've just got this rhythm down."

Long is normally the pacer, but Sharpe will set the pace on occasion. The only rules are that they sprint across the finish line — and no clotheslining of runners who try to pass.

"We always win our division," Long said, laughing.

Long jokes around, but Sharpe trusts him implicitly, and Long understands the responsibility.

"It's just a blessing to have a friend like Jon," Long said. "We joke around a lot, but when you get down to it, it's another gift from God that you can do something like that. In essence, I'm helping lead him, but he's also helping lead me a lot of times, too.

"He helps me see life better by watching him go through his struggles and trials. We can get together and pray together about something or cry together over something and just share everything. He's taught me that when I get a little hangnail, it's nothing compared to what he's going through."

Long is a liquor salesman, and Sharpe works for Parkview Behavioral Center as an individual and family therapist, but in their minds, they are still 10-year-olds running around before dinner.

"Sports is still as much a love for me now as it was when we were growing up," Sharpe said.

When will they stop?

"I hope we don't ever stop," Sharpe said. "After we die, I think."

"Then we'll do it up there, too," Long said.

CHAPTER 34
Seifert massages his way to success
Published Aug. 23, 2000, in The News-Sentinel

Several years ago, Tom Seifert used to give massages to friends who traveled extensively. The friends encouraged him to give up his job delivering dairy products and become a massage therapist.

At first, he wasn't sure it was the right decision.

"I was really sweating," he said. "God has blessed me in a real special way to be able to do this. It's been amazing."

Seifert went to school in Marion, Ind., in 1986 and opened a private practice as a massage therapist in 1988. A year later, he worked the RCA Hardcourts Championships in Indianapolis when tennis star Pete Sampras walked in. It was the first of many meetings with famous athletes.

A few years later, Seifert was hired as part of the Davis Cup team by Sampras' coach.

In less than three weeks, he'll rub out knots and kinks for the U.S. tennis players competing at the Sydney Olympics

"I'm just really thankful for everybody who has supported me and my family," the 48-year-old Seifert said. "It's a great opportunity to represent your country. It's just an incredible honor."

Seifert's trek to Sydney really started in 1994 when he joined the U.S. Davis Cup team at the behest of the late Tom Gullickson. Since then, his travels have included India, the Netherlands,

Sweden, Germany, Italy, Russia, Brazil and France. But don't ask him what his favorite site was at each stop. Seifert's sightseeing is confined to whatever he can see on the ride from the hotel to the arena because of the team's busy schedule.

He has worked with stars such as Michael Chang, Todd Martin, the Jensen brothers, MaliVai Washington, Andre Agassi, John McEnroe and Sampras, becoming friends with most. Seifert has had a front-row seat for some of the most intense sporting competitions in the world.

"It's a little bit of high stress for me, too," he said. "Anytime you walk in and work on a million-dollar player — $2 million, $3 million, $4 million, whatever these guys are worth — you've got a lot at stake. Your career's at stake, your reputation is at stake, so you want to make sure you do what those guys want."

Seifert believes he can help improve a player's performance by as much as 20 percent, especially in helping prevent injuries. It must work, because some players have paid him to travel with them to tournaments.

And he has some great stories. One time in Moscow, he and Sampras raced around the city in the back of a police car. A trip that should have taken 20 minutes lasted only nine.

"The guy drove like Jeff Gordon," Seifert said. "We were taking curves sliding, drove up on the sidewalk, and he was driving in the opposing lane. Pete and I thought we were dead. I don't think Pete will ever forget that ride."

Another time Seifert, admittedly a complete duffer as a player, picked up a racket and dared Sampras to hit his best serve past him. Four times, Sampras wound up and smacked the ball 125 mph. Seifert ticked one of them.

In one of the few other times he has picked up a racket during a Davis Cup tour, Seifert decided to hit a little with Jim Courier, who was practicing. He didn't move fast enough on one play, and a Courier forehand blasted Seifert on the thigh. The welt was still there a week after he came home.

"And my game still stinks to this day," Seifert said.

The only drawback to traveling is that his wife, Pam, and sons Garren, 10, and Gavin, 1, don't go with him. They do see the pictures of the famous people that Seifert hangs on the wall of his office in Fort Wayne, Ind.

"Basically, people see them and just sit there looking at them with their mouths shut," Seifert said. "I hope they think it's kind of cool. I'm sure some of them don't believe it. There are times I don't, either."

CHAPTER 35
Those he mentored will never forget Larry Westendorf
Published April 22, 2005, in The News-Sentinel

Valedictorian Leah Heaston wrote in her address to the 1997 University of Saint Francis graduating class:

"Throughout the last four years, there has been one person whom I have learned to admire for his dedication to the students, to the athletes and to Saint Francis College. I cannot adequately express how much this person has meant to me."

On Saturday, Larry Westendorf, 66, will be inducted into the University of Saint Francis Athletic Hall of Fame just four days before he undergoes major surgery in Indianapolis because of cancer.

Every few weeks, a new letter will arrive for Westendorf, always with a card inside wishing him good luck in the upcoming challenge.

The messages inside say more than any card ever could.

"You are one of the very few people who has helped me to be the person I am today, and for that I am eternally grateful," Jennie (Buchan) Knepper wrote. "How wonderful for you to know that I am certainly not the only child/person/player you have had the same effect on. Thank you so much for all the wonderful, heartfelt memories. I feel confidence that with your strength of character, perseverance and prayer, you will get through this."

As he talks about the letters, Westendorf's eyes start misting and his bottom lip starts quivering.

"It's what the chemo does to you," he finally says after a deep breath. "It makes you more emotional."

The doctors are pessimistic, but Westendorf is not. He's already told friends he's shooting to be back at work two weeks after the surgery.

"I really believe that I've had a perfect life," he said. "I think that God is saying, 'OK, Larry, you're OK, but you aren't as damn perfect as you think you are, and I gotta throw a little stuff at you, and here it is.' OK, I can handle that."

He has always approached life with that positive attitude and tried to pass it on to every athlete on any team he has coached.

Because he was so successful in doing so, he'll have hundreds of people praying for his recovery, dozens will be there for his induction, and more letters are coming.

* * *

Heaston: "When we see the respect he has for female athletes, we know he has God in his heart. When we see his wife and family at athletic events, we know he has family in his heart. When we see him permit his athletes to miss athletic events to attend classes they simply cannot afford to miss, we know he has academics in his heart."

Maybe no male in Fort Wayne, Ind., history has done as much for female athletes as Westendorf. Because his wife needed a place to play, he formed a softball league in nearby New Haven in the early 1960s, even though he had no formal coaching training. When he started coaching girls basketball at St. Charles Borromeo Catholic School in the 1970s, he was the first male coach of a girls team in the Catholic Youth Organization. He has no idea how many championships his teams won, but they won plenty.

"My problem was I never kept records for that stuff," he said. "People would ask, 'How was your season?' and I would say, 'I won't know until all the (high school) freshmen try out and we see how many make it next fall.' We did our job if eight of our 10 kids tried out and made it somewhere."

In 1989 he went to the University of Saint Francis as an assistant basketball coach. It was supposed to be a paid position, but the check never arrived. The next year, he was named the head coach with a full-time salary of $3,500. Taking over a team that had won just seven games, he built the Cougars into an NAIA National Tournament squad in 1995, the first of eight straight tournament berths.

In 1992, he became the school's athletic director of female sports and later took up coaching the softball team — after building the field. When officials wanted to dump the tennis team because of a lack of interest, he took that over, too, often holding tennis practice in the morning, basketball practice in the early evening and softball practice late at night. During his spare time, he'd do the laundry, clean the gym, teach a physical education class or run his contracting business. Oh, and he'd live a normal life with his wife, Mary Jane, and their five children.

* * *

Heaston: "His willingness to share and to be fair with everyone. His smile. His ability to spread happiness to others. But above all, his honesty. As athletes, we know he will always be there for us. We know he will love us no matter what the score at the end of the game. We know he will bend over backward to help and take care of us. He will be there to encourage, to support, to hold us when we fall, and to push us when we need the courage to move forward."

He could never ask for anything for himself, but Westendorf can beg for someone else's cause. When he started, the women's basketball players at Saint Francis were given $10 toward buying shoes. Within a few years, the men's coaches were complaining because the female teams always seemed to have the most money. The school later added women's soccer under Westendorf's direction. After some personnel moves, Saint

Francis eventually asked him to leave in 1999. Indiana Tech university coach Gary Cobb asked him to join his staff.

"He said he wanted to take some time off, but the real reason is he didn't want to coach against those kids (from Saint Francis)," Cobb said. "That made me want him even more."

Westendorf's strength was working with athletes one-on-one in the field and in the gym, where he used sports as a tool to teach players about life.

Yes, deep down, he knows — partly because those players are so willing to tell him. He believed in everybody, and now everybody is rallying for him, coming to him with their support, their prayers, their belief in him. Even though he's no longer their coach, Westendorf is still teaching them about teamwork and life.

"If God's not ready for me, I'll be fine," he said. "I'm not ready to give in."
His first grandchild, Alyssa, was born 10 months ago and is just starting to learn to walk. As he did for hundreds of others girls, he wants to show her how to play.

"I have to stick around, because I've got a lot of things to teach her."

Heaston: "This man, Larry Westendorf, is the one who taught me God, family, academics and then athletics. To the graduating class of 1997, I challenge each of you to follow the building blocks and the values he has taught me. If we all can learn to share, to be fair, to be honest, to spread happiness, to put God and family above all else, we can make the world a better place — just as Larry Westendorf has done."

CHAPTER 36
Rugby helped Mark Elrod save his life
Published July 16, 2014, in The News-Sentinel

At age 25, Mark Elrod loved rugby so much he walked away rather than embarrass the sport.

At age 42, Mark Elrod loved rugby so much he changed and saved his life to play it again.

When Elrod was an 18-year-old senior at Woodlan High School, he was a backup offensive lineman at 166 pounds. He always had the aggressiveness and attitude to play much bigger than his size, though, especially the attitude, which is why he was a backup.

To fill the competitive void after high school, he joined the Fort Wayne Rugby Club at age 20. He loved the passion, ferociousness and camaraderie of the game. He could be free on the field, pushing, pounding and screaming with his buddies, who all understood without ever having to talk about it. No one needed padding.

Rugby, Elrod says, is more about the people who play than the sport itself. They all love the bond they form, which is often more fun than the games, because there's no clock winding down on friendship.

Then Elrod's body started to grow into his persona. He'd eat anything and wouldn't stop. Each night, he'd drink 2 liters of pop and consume junk food or whatever was around.

He finally reached 405 pounds and walked away from rugby and his friends.

"I just couldn't do it," he said. "I was too big and too out of shape. I just got obsessed with food and overate and didn't exercise. It's depressing to me to think about what kind of person I could have been if I hadn't gotten into that mode."

He couldn't run or compete. Feeling out of place, he stayed away from rugby for 15 years. Part of his life that he loved was just gone, shoved to the back of his mind to be forgotten.

Life continued. He got married, started his own landscaping business and drove a school bus. He also coached PAL (Police Athletic League) football for 21 years.

Eventually, he decided to have bariatric surgery and went into Lutheran Hospital's Health Weight Management program. He became a model patient, eventually getting as low as 194 pounds. When that weight didn't feel right, he settled in around 225 pounds, and he's kept within 10 pounds ever since. Elrod thought he was busy enough that the competitive itch and his love for rugby would stay buried. But deep loves are never buried for good no matter how thick the scar tissue.

About five years ago, a year after his surgery, Elrod and his wife, Jennifer, were watching TV and saw a news report about the Fort Wayne Rugby Club's 40th anniversary. Jennifer had never seen Mark play but knew he was just nuts enough to try it when he vowed to get into shape to play again. He started training.

"Everybody has a craziness that they need to get out every now and then," she said.

The first time Elrod ran onto the field, some of his old buddies didn't recognize him. They couldn't match up the smaller man with their memories.

"He played with my dad, and I knew him as a bigger guy," Chuck Geyer said. "When he came back after he lost all that weight, he came up and gave me a hug, and I said, 'Mark? Is that you?' He looked awesome!"

The players could have crushed him if they had rejected him, said he was too old or acted like they simply didn't know him anymore. Instead, they all embraced him with no hesitation.

Elrod was a new man, but he still teared up that day for what he had lost and what he had regained. The emotion just overtook him.

"I'm an old guy and I'm really not that good of a rugby player," he said. "I just do it because I enjoy it. It's so neat, because they accept me into the program and let me come back and play with them. It's so neat that they accepted me when I hadn't played in 15 years."

That's just rugby, though, the little sport that needs everybody to be successful. Everyone sacrifices and suffers to play. There are always bruises and a need for more players, so even the guys who are hurt keep going. It's a subculture of the overlooked athletes who play simply for the joy. There's always respect for anyone who pulls on a jersey and a pair of boots.

"The cool thing about rugby is that it's a lifelong sport," FWRC president Sam DiFilippo said. "We're one of those sports that you can take a five-, six-year break from it and come back and play if you want to give it another run. We're only as good as the guys who came before us."

Now Elrod is 47 years old, holding steady at 225 pounds and playing in six or seven matches a year. He's blowing up players

20 years younger — when he can catch them. He's again letting out his wild side during the competitions. He knows he's going to be hurting afterward, but it's worth it.

"I would have never told him, 'No, you're not going out there,' but I did tell him to stay away from the ball so he didn't get a broken leg," Jennifer said with a laugh. "He's got a broken rib now, but he can still work, so it's all good. If you are going to be a grown man and go play little-boy's games, then take the pain and act like it doesn't bother you."

Elrod suffered a broken rib and a black eye two months ago during a match, but it's a pair of broken toes suffered on the job that slows him down now.

"I think he can play for another five or six years," Geyer said. "It's crazy because you see a bunch of the older guys who come out and get one game and then they disappear for another two or three years. It's different with Mark. It's like he's young again because he lost all the weight and he's a new man. He can go for a whole 80 minutes."

And then he'll talk about the match for another 80 minutes with his buddies. He credits God and Jennifer for his rebirth, figuring either could have taken his life away when he was 405 pounds but they stuck with him. And so have his buddies.

"I explain it to people this way. I missed out for 15 years of my life," he said. "I'm trying to make up that time. That really gives me my mojo. I missed the socials and I missed the guys even though I didn't always get along with them. I just missed the camaraderie of good men. Now, this has given me something to live for, something to work for. I still want to play into my 50s."

That's how much he loves rugby.

CHAPTER 37
Driver has an interesting life off the track
Published July 20, 2017, in The News-Sentinel

Of all the drivers racing this weekend at Baer Field Motorsports Park, Sam Tolley might have the most interesting trek to the track. He might even have had the most interesting life so far.

According to his birth certificate, Tolley was born 35 years ago in Fort Wayne, but by age 3, he was living in the New Mexico Baptist Children's home, the state's longest-running orphanage. He left at age 16 and was taken in by Roger and Gayleen Saylor.

"I'm 16, you're a young kid and you think you know it all," Tolley said. "Growing up the way I grew up, it was kind of hard for me to have people telling me how and what to do. I wasn't used to a family structure. When I was 17, I got up one day and said I'd had enough of this, and I was going to make something of myself."

After a few odd jobs didn't work out, Tolley enlisted in the Army. During a 10-year career, he made three tours in Iraq, serving 4 1/2 years there, and one in Colombia, earning a Purple Heart and 13 other medals. He was a ranger and a sniper, reaching the rank of staff sergeant.

While stationed at Fort Hood in Texas, he was also a racer at small dirt tracks in Waco, Lubbock and Kileen, competing for five years starting at age 22.

"It was kind of what the Army didn't know didn't hurt them type of deal," Tolley said.

He left the Army in December 2009 at age 27, moving to Clovis,

N.M., where he wanted to get into business driving a semitrailer to haul cattle. He met his wife, Meghan, saying she was the best-looking short-order cook he'd ever seen, and she took pity upon him.

Then they decided to try living in northeast Indiana, working for the Line Star Calf Depot in Newville.

"When we moved up here, we literally stopped the truck on the side of the road," he said. "I said, 'Let's turn back,' and she said, 'We're doing this.' It's amazing, because at that point and time, I could have changed my path, and I thank God every day for my wife being behind me. She made a very good decision for us and our life."

Part of that included reconnecting with the Saylors. They'd had no contact for about 12 years, and Tolley had even tried reaching out to his birth parents with no success.

"Something was telling me this is where I needed to be, and I battled with it, and I didn't want to do it, but I moved here, and it's probably the third-best thing that's ever happened to me," he said, mentioning his wife as first and his two daughters and son as the second. "Roger and Gayleen (had) put up with my antics and my flat-out disrespect sometimes. I'm not proud of some of the things I did when I was young, but they have done a very good job of molding me into who I am, just like my wife. I am a project of my wife and Roger and Gayleen. It's not all me. It's the people I'm around. A lot of people have helped turn me into who I am today."

And that includes being a local racer. When promoter Dave Muzzillo took over BFMP in 2015, Tolley climbed back into a car, buying a super late model from Tommy Cook and picking the number "8jr." to honor Roger Saylor's No. 8.

Now Tolley is one of the few drivers who compete on both the asphalt and dirt tracks at BFMP.

"What I learned from asphalt will make my dirt driving even better, because it's about patience," Tolley said. "The saying is that you drive a dirt car with your foot and an asphalt car with your brain. You use the throttle a lot more in dirt cars, and you don't have to be nearly as consistent, just use a lot more motor. Now I like the asphalt just as much as dirt."

Tolley's life has been an amazing, unpredictable ride so far.

"A lot of people I grew up with are either (into) drugs or in and out of jail," Tolley said. "To be where I'm at today is ... I have bad days like everybody else, but my bad days are not nearly as tough as what I've already went through. The biggest thing I've noticed about kids who grew up like I did is they often use the situation like a crutch. I've learned to take a lot of the negatives and turn it into a positive. It always fuels me to be the best I possibly can be no matter what I'm doing."

CHAPTER 38
After picking himself up, Gerard Willis refuses to go down again
Published Sept. 6, 2017, in The News-Sentinel

When he moves, even as little as sitting up in a chair, some part of Gerard Willis' body creaks or snaps. He calls it his popcorn sounds because some joint is always popping.

He's 48 with the body of a 78-year-old. After a 17-year Army stint, his injuries include a traumatic brain injury (TBI), which can affect balance, stability and memory; arthritis in his hands, knees and back; degenerative disk disease; fibromyalgia; and he thinks his Veterans Administration doctors are going to give him bad news any day about his neck.

It's all just more popcorn to him.

But he also wants to try to participate in a triathlon as part of a new program that Turnstone Center for Children and Adults with Disabilities is offering. A triathlon includes bicycling, running and swimming.

"I've never done it before," he said. "I enjoy life, and I don't want to say, 'I wish I had done that when I had the opportunity.' If I have the opportunity to do things, I want to do them."

The amazing part is that only a handful of years ago, Willis didn't care if he ever did anything again.

In 2009, he was serving in Anniston, Ala., and was driving to work in the afternoon. He was looking down at an accident at the bottom of a hill that had traffic backed up, when another car slammed into his from behind.

"I got rear-ended by a kid who was not even paying attention and never even touched his breaks," Willis said.

The car was totaled and so almost was Willis, who was knocked unconscious and suffered a severe concussion and the TBI. He was assigned restrictive duty for three months while doing physical therapy and testing to try to reduce his headaches.

Willis said when he first got out of the service, doctors were throwing pills at him, and he was basically in a walking, medicated coma for a few years in his hometown of Baltimore.

"I was a recluse. I stayed in the house, I kept the lights dark for the first five years," he said. "I was married at the time, and my wife didn't know what to do with me. I was in constant pain, and my head would swell up and I didn't know what to do. I was literally waiting to die."

Then one day in 2011, he offered a friend a place to stay, and that person cleaned his house out of anything valuable. So frustrated, he began praying.

"I said, 'God, I don't want to be this way any longer. I'm trying to do the right thing, I'm trying to help somebody out, and they turn around and bite me in the hand. How do I stop being like this? What do I need to do?'

"He was like, 'It's time for you to change,'" Willis said. "I needed to step out on faith."

At one time during his Army years, Willis had trained in Indiana and decided he liked the people. He had a friend in Fort Wayne who offered to take him in, so he moved here. In 2012, the local VA Hospital suggested he try Turnstone, which was starting a new program called "Healthy Minds, Healthy Bodies" that was targeted to veterans, feeling the camaraderie and fellowship would help provide inspiration.

Willis started working out with the group and eventually knocked off 60 pounds. He started to feel more normal in 2013, both physically and spiritually, and became a bigger part of the community. He served as commander of the Disabled American Veterans chapter for two years and also is part of the Allen

County Council of Veterans.

He can walk, though he sometimes needs a cane on bad days. He's remarried and can provide counsel to other veterans facing problems. He loves new challenges, which Turnstone is pretty good at providing. He's tried kayaking, air rifle, archery, cycling, powerlifting, shot put and discus, and he even won some medals at the Valor Games in Chicago.

"Gerard will step up and try anything," said Turnstone's sports and recreation coordinator, Kevin Hughes. "He really likes to be exposed to new activities. Many times, we'll be trying something, and he'll always step up and give it a shot."

It's quite a difference from someone who, a few years ago, was waiting to die.

"I had hope because I stayed positive," he said. "You always want to have a positive outlook on everything, because if you walk in with a negative attitude, nine times out of 10 you are going to get a negative attitude.

"For the most part, my injuries are invisible. From the time I wake up in the morning my body aches, and it takes me an hour just to get up out of bed. It's disheartening, because I don't like feeling like this every day, but it's the only way I can make it through my day, knowing that if I don't get up, I'm giving up."

CHAPTER 39
Army veteran and Boston winner enjoys sharing his story
Published April 17, 2013, in The News-Sentinel

Tom Davis is proving God creates miracles.

The United States Army staff sergeant was serving in Iraq on June 3, 2006, when the truck he was riding in triggered a roadside bomb. Riding shotgun, Davis lost his left leg above the knee, broke both forearms, fractured his right knee and a vertebra in his back, and cracked some bones in his head. He also was diagnosed with traumatic brain injury and post-traumatic stress disorder.

He recovered in the hospital for six or seven weeks and then spent 15 months rehabilitating at Walter Reed Army Medical Center. Now age 35, he lives in Fremont, Ind., with his wife, Jamie, and their children, ages 11, 7, 5 and 3.

Recently, Davis told a crowd of kids at Turnstone Center for Children and Adults with Disabilities how they can overcome what everyone else may see as debilitating injuries, diseases and birth problems and still become anything they want. Monday morning, he proved it by winning the Boston Marathon in the handcycling division.

"What I love most about it is being able to go to elementary schools, middle schools and youth groups and talk to them about it," Davis said.

Now, he's really got something to talk to them about.

About a mile into his first Boston race, Davis passed the man who would finish second, putting a full five minutes of distance between them by the time he cruised across the finish line in 1 hour, 17 minutes and 59 seconds.

An avid runner when he was growing up in Reading, Mich.,

Davis said he tried using a handcycle as part of his therapy at Walter Reed.

He didn't get his first one until 2008, which he rode while he was serving as an instructor at Fort Benning, Ga. The bike sat in his shed for quite a while because he got into weight lifting instead.

"Then I felt like God was calling me to start handcycling," Davis said.

He started with a couple of races in 2011, and 2012 was his first full year in competition. His cardio work from running and power from weightlifting meant handcycling was the perfect format for him.

"I've always been a runner, and once I got hurt, I couldn't run anymore, so being able to get into a sport where I can go fast ... the speed and the competition is what I love," he said.

After trying two races in 2011, Davis put together an 18-race schedule last year and lost only twice. His focus was on the Paralympic Games, but he finished second in his division at the United States trials and did not qualify for London. Then he started focusing on the Boston Marathon.

You know what he's really looking forward to? A former high school classmate has invited him to speak at her school next month.

"Last year, I was all about racing and the whole Paralympic thing," he said. "This year, it's like God is asking, 'What are you going to do with it besides just winning races?' I'm going to find out."

CHAPTER 40
Alexandra Alderdice showed true courage facing mother's death
Published Dec. 14, 2016, in The News-Sentinel

Throughout the gymnastics season last year, Alexandra Alderdice worked at improving her uneven bars routine. The problem was some days during practice, the Carroll High School freshman could hit her giants — a swinging, fully extended rotation around the top bar — but she couldn't successfully complete the move during meets. As the state tournament approached, the Chargers needed the points Alderdice could score with a successful routine.

"She was one of the hardest-working girls every day, and she did routine after routine, giant after giant," Carroll coach Rosemary Scheele said. "She'd do 20 sets of it in practice, but she would go to the meets, and she couldn't do her giants. I knew eventually she would do it."

Though the Chargers placed third in the Concordia Sectional to advance to the Huntington North Regional, Alderdice continued to struggle. Scheele kept her in the spot, leading off as the first of four Chargers in the event. Scheele knew there was something else going on in Alderdice's life.

Off and on for about 10 years, Alderdice's mother, Kristina, had been battling breast cancer. A fighter, she regularly underwent chemotherapy, but the disease kept returning. Wanting to protect her children and allow them to live as normally as possible, she didn't always keep them fully informed about her health.

About halfway through last season, Kristina went for an

extended stay in the hospital, and that's when Alexandra understood something was seriously wrong. During the last meet she attended, Kristina talked about how the cancer had attacked her liver and she felt bloated.

Along with her brother Charlie, Alexandra stayed with different family members and friends, attending school and then gymnastics practice before visiting their mother in the hospital each night.

"At meets and practices, I tried not to think about it, because then it got in the way," Alderdice said. "Gymnastics has always been there so I could get away from everything else that was happening, but also to go have fun with my teammates. She always told me I could do anything I put my mind to and never pressured me. She was always there for me."

Though her teammates knew what was going on, Alderdice didn't talk about her mother, so her coaches and teammates let her be. She knew she could turn to them but maintained her usual reserved personality.

"We knew it was bothering her, but she gave it everything she had," Scheele said. "She would come to the gym, and we felt like she needed to be in her gymnastics family world and to have a relief from the stresses she had lived with most of her life."

But how could Alderdice hold up under these conditions? Not only was the gymnastics season peaking, but this time, Kristina was not bouncing back and coming home. The future was incredibly uncertain, and how could she find a way to compete, attend school and possibly say goodbye to her mother at the same time? There was too much for any freshman to handle without help.

"I just remember nighttime was my quiet time, and I would dive into the Word," she said. "I have a ton of devotion books that Mom had, and it really helped me. It was having confidence in myself. I knew I was going to be OK either way, that even though I might not do well, I knew I'd still be OK because of my faith, being strong in God. Not only did my faith keep me strong, but the strength that my mom had helped me to keep pressing on during the difficult time. One of her favorite phrases was, 'Don't be a Debby Downer.'"

Alexandra also reached out to her teammates, who were always there to listen or help out with a ride or a place to stay. They kept encouraging, and she kept working to nail those giants. It also helped that no high school sport involves more hugs than gymnastics.

Kristina went into the hospital for the final time the week before sectionals. Alexandra prayed the whole time for her mother to fully recover, but during the week before the regional, she was told the situation was dire. She still wanted to compete — for herself, her teammates and her family.

With her cousin, Emma Starks, Skyping back to Kristina in her hospital room, Alderdice scored a season-high 8.75 on the balance beam to place 12th, but the bars were still to come. After a little wave to Kristina via Emma filming from the corner, Alderdice attacked the apparatus, conquering her giants and scoring a season-high 8.225 to place 19th. Her smile scored even higher.

"I think you had a guardian angel with you," Scheele told Alderdice after a congratulatory hug.

Somehow, she had overcome so much to succeed in the big moment.

"I had to do it for my team because they were counting on me," Alderdice said simply.

But completing her goal and the end of the season also meant she could relax and accept what was happening with her mother, who passed away six days later. Alderdice learned so much from the experience, surviving a test most don't go through until they are much older.

"I have learned that when I am weak, I need to declare that I am strong (Joel 3:10). My mom taught me that," she said. "It's kind of hard."

Another favorite verse is Isaiah 40:31: "But those who hope in the Lord will renew their strength. They will soar on wings like eagles; they will run and not grow weary, they will walk and not be faint."

"This verse has taught me a lot about hoping in the Lord in difficult circumstances," Alderdice said.

Though the mourning continues, Alexandra and Charlie are living with their aunt and uncle. It's almost time for gymnastics season again, and this time she's working hard on a new vault. Life is mostly back to normal, as normal as it is for any high school sophomore. Alderdice is getting used to and liking a little bit of normal with hopes for a strong sophomore season.

"It's different every day," she said. "It's like a routine type of thing, and we're just working it out. Every day can be different for me. I can have good or bad moments now, where before I had good and bad days. I could be happy on the outside, but inside, not really. Now we're all working at it together, doing it together."

CHAPTER 41
The Gospel according to Mom
Published in the Bethlehem Lutheran Church Messenger

For decades, whenever I had a problem, my mother would say, "Give it to God" in prayer. No matter how big or little the problem, that was always Mom's answer.

Fine, it sounds great, but it's not that easy. How exactly do you do that?

Ok, so I recently learned it might just be that easy. I was the one making it hard — of course. I won't tell you whom I get my stubbornness from.

Anyway, one Sunday afternoon, I had a "Eureka!" moment during our Bible study led by my father. I can't remember exactly how the topic came up, but Joyce Knipstein — my second mom — told a story about how when her daughter Theresa was in the second or third grade, they built a prayer box.

"Theresa was having trouble about how to give something over to God in prayer without worrying about it," Joyce said. "How do you do that? I'm a visual person, and I said, 'Let's make a prayer box, and everything we have problems with and need to pray about, we'll put on a piece of paper and put it in that box and then forget about it.'

"She was much more of a visual person than I am, and she

needed to write it down. Once she wrote it down, it was out of her mind and she wasn't stewing about it. Once she didn't think about it anymore to that depth, the things God wanted her to do became a lot clearer. We're giving it to the Lord. It's in His hands, not yours anymore. You can go on and live life without getting yourself all upset and things like that."

So they took a box and decorated it with paper, cut a hole in the top and placed it in Theresa's room. Whenever she had a problem, she'd write it down on a piece of paper and put it in God's prayer box.

"I tried to reiterate that it was between her and God," Joyce said. "If she was having a problem, she could come to us and talk about it. She could also put it in the box, give it to God and let go of it. I'd say, 'It's in the box, and there's nothing you can do about it. You've given it to God, and now you have to wait for His answer.'

"Not surprisingly, that solved many problems. Sometimes, Theresa solved the problem because God gave her the wisdom, which she was able to see and understand because she wasn't worrying so much."

But where did Joyce get the idea for the box? Was it something her family had done?

"Probably the Lord," she said. "It's not mine, God did it. It was, 'How are we going to do this? Lord, help us when we say our prayers.' I think it was sort of, 'God, what do you want me to do? I don't understand. Here it is, you gotta help me with this.'

"It's just something that came to mind … because she loves to write. She's a great writer. She can do that and put it in the box and give it to the Lord. At the time, it's out of your mind. You know you've given it to God and he's working on it."

Without a doubt, one of the hardest things in life is having the patience to let God work things out, but I realized this is one way to do that. It's so simple, it's perfect. If you'd rather not use a box, write the problems down and put them in your Bible.

"A lot of people will look back six months later and see that their prayers have been answered," Joyce's husband, Ken, said.

"As I said this many times, it wasn't us who raised our children, it was God," Joyce said. "We all made mistakes, but it was God who gave us the common sense to get the job done."

CHAPTER 42
Sister's love keeps coach in the game
Published Jan. 27, 2005, in The News-Sentinel

Even though her Jeep Wrangler's radio needs to be fixed, Laura Douglas doesn't mind the long drives each week for recruiting. It gives her time to reflect and talk with her sister, whom she shared a bedroom with for 16 years.

Now they talk about their parents, Laura's new job, daily life and their brother Jared. The funny thing is, their mother used to tell Laura all the time that she should spend more time with Sarah, but their schedules rarely meshed.

"I just hope that she's OK and everything is good for her," Laura Douglas said.

Sarah Douglas died on May 26, 2002, when she was involved in a traffic accident that killed three people. Her death took a tremendous emotional toll on her family and her co-workers at Indiana Tech, where she was the assistant controller and soon-to-be assistant softball coach. She was known for having a quiet, down-to-earth personality, always accomplishing her goals and liking to work with students.

Sarah was 24 and, according to Laura, the perfect big sister.

"I remember when I was in kindergarten, she threw a kid up against a wall who was teasing me," Laura said. "She was always looking out for me. She took care of me when she was here, and she still takes care of me."

Now Laura Douglas, 26, is putting together the first Indiana Tech women's volleyball team since the 1980s, and her heart says Sarah had a hand in her getting the job. Sarah was always Laura's biggest fan, even though Laura was the more widely recognized athlete. Even when the younger Laura got more playing time, Sarah was always supportive, always proud of her sister.

After her graduation from Indiana University-Purdue University Fort Wayne, Laura taught first grade at St. John's Lutheran School and coached the Elmhurst High School girls volleyball team for two years. She decided to leave that position last spring with hopes of teaching in a public school and eventually achieving her ultimate goal of coaching in college. Despite sending out countless resumes, there was no new job. By the beginning of August, Douglas was getting desperate.

"I was so down that week," Douglas said. "I prayed, 'What am I going to do, God? Maybe teaching isn't what I'm supposed to be doing.'"

She decided to go back to school and study engineering. At the same time, Indiana Tech Athletic Director Dan Kline was calling IPFW men's volleyball coach Arnie Ball to ask for potential women's volleyball candidates. Among others, Ball mentioned Douglas, who played volleyball for four years and basketball for three at IPFW, where she was known for her work ethic, intelligence and making the most of her many abilities.

As soon as Kline heard Douglas' name, he remembered Sarah and knew he had to call. Sarah Douglas was an academic All-America softball pitcher at Indiana Tech who would often bring her little sister around.

"Everything about Sarah was first-class, and her death just stunned us," Kline said. "The first time I sat down to talk to Laura, I knew she was the one we needed."

Douglas was delighted and realized she had just landed her dream job, even though she's working long hours putting together a budget and a schedule, serving as assistant women's basketball coach and also working as the director of the school's new wellness center.

She believes that God, with a little nudge from Sarah, has led her to where she should be.

"I feel like I got the opportunity that she never had," Laura said. "I get to carry on her glory and do something that I know she would have enjoyed, too. (Indiana Tech) was my sister's passion, and I think she wants me to be here. I think this was meant to be."

And because everyone knew Sarah, Laura had a head start in her new career. Everyone feels like they already know Laura because of Sarah's reputation.

"She laid the groundwork for the Douglas family here, and I just have to follow that," Laura said. "I feel blessed and honored to be here.

"I told her, 'Thanks, Sarah, you have definitely helped me out again.' She took care of me again."

UPDATE: In 2013, Douglas, now Laura Stegall, started the Daytona State women's volleyball team, where she's been the coach for six years. Her oldest daughter, Sarah Anne, was named for her sister.
"She's about to turn 9," Stegall said. "In many ways, she reminds me of my sister, (in) personality and appearance."

CHAPTER 43
Kerry Inglis' faith provides Senior Day inspiration
Published Oct. 29, 2008, in The News-Sentinel

When she woke up Sunday morning, Kerry Inglis prayed, "OK, God, please make this a good day."

There haven't been too many good days during Inglis' soccer career at the University of Notre Dame. Despite being a top-notch recruit, the Snider High School product suffered a severe ankle injury during her first day of practice as a freshman and has played sparingly during her career.

Sunday was Senior Day for the undefeated and No. 1 Irish, and Inglis, 21, thought she might get to play a little against Big East foe Seton Hall. What happened became one of the most inspirational stories in a place that is famous for them.

Irish coach Randy Waldrum decided to start all the seniors, making this the first start and only the 18th game of Inglis' career. As assistant coach Ken Nuber walked up to give Inglis a hug at the Senior Day ceremonies, he whispered, "Score" in her ear. Inglis said she would try her best.

That's basically all she's been able to do for four years. She was already trying to learn a new position going into her freshman season when she caught her right ankle while trying to make a tackle.

"There are a lot of sprained ankles, and usually you can wobble around," she said. "I remember thinking, 'Kerry, don't be a wimp, it's your first day,' but I couldn't put any weight on it."

Though the ankle didn't heal, Inglis tried playing through it, getting into eight matches. Then she pulled a tendon during warm-ups for a game against Providence to end her season. Eventually, doctors told her she had a defective bone in her ankle and that she needed postseason surgery, so she sat out her sophomore season. When the healing didn't progress far enough, she had another surgery in January 2007 and came back to play in six games.

"The sad thing is when we recruited her, she had so much potential," Waldrum said. "We had these great visions for her. She's basically playing on a reconstructed ankle, and she lost that explosiveness and quickness. You feel so bad for her."

But Inglis, a history/political science major, never complained publicly and kept working on her rehabilitation, often when no one else was around. She knew that to have a chance to play at

Notre Dame, she had to be 100 percent, and it started to sink in that she never would be.

"There have been 100 times when I wanted to walk away from it," she said. "It wasn't working, and I was unhappy with the fact that I couldn't do the things I should be able to do.

"I felt like I was letting people down when I got hurt, but at the same time, I didn't really have any choice but to keep going. Some people have asked me how I keep doing it, and to me, it doesn't seem like I really had a choice. I couldn't step away from it. I had to finish it out."

So she kept trying, kept working with the trainers and her teammates, and finally, Sunday was her chance. Waldrum moved her from outside defender to forward, figuring it would be easier for her to make the necessary moves on her ankle.

The amazing part, Waldrum said, is that few people realize what Inglis has gone through, because she doesn't talk about it around the program. She never lets on how much it has hurt to lose her dream.

"She's one of those kids that the rest of the team can look at when things aren't going their way," he said. "She's been an unbelievable role model for the team, the ultimate team player."

On Sunday, the program gave her a little back. About 11 minutes into the match, fellow senior Brittany Bock kicked a cross from the right side that found Inglis near the far post, where she was able to tap the ball into the net. It was the first goal of her career.

"At first, I didn't even realize what had happened," Inglis said. "I couldn't believe it. I walked back to midfield, and I looked over at the bench, and they were still screaming and jumping up and down. I almost lost it right there, but I kept thinking, 'It's in the middle of a game, and I can't do that.'"

The day got even better when Inglis scored again in the 84th minute of a 6-0 win, but she still kept her emotions in as teammates and parents mobbed her after the game. She kept waiting, figuring once she started crying, she'd never stop.

"I couldn't have asked God for anything more," Inglis said. "It's been hard. My faith has always been very important to me, especially in high school, but because of what has happened here, I've gotten a little bit bitter.
"Sometimes it's hard to understand the full perspective of things that happen. There are so many struggles in life, I always feel so guilty for being upset. Some people have cancer or can't walk, and mine is just an ankle injury."

So when she prayed Sunday night, Inglis almost couldn't find the words.

"It was just, 'Thank you, God,'" she said.

CHAPTER 44
Iric Headley overcame his own troubles to help others
Published Oct. 30, 2017, on News-Sentinel.com

Before he moved to Fort Wayne, Ind., from Trinidad and Tobago at age 11, Iric Headley said he had never seen a white person. Then at age 14, standing on his front porch, he met one of Fort Wayne's biggest drug dealers.

"My life just changed from that point on," he said. "From 16 to 19, my goal was to be the biggest drug dealer in Fort Wayne. I was into music, too — gangster rapper. All the filthy stuff you hear on the radio? Killing, women and drugs, I was at the top of that world, man."

But God had other plans for Headley, and he met Pastor Anthony Payton, who'd had a terrible past as well before turning his own life around. Headley finally listened.

"I just lost everything and gave my life to Christ at that point," Headley said.

Today, selected by Mayor Tom Henry, Headley serves as the executive director of Fort Wayne United, a program targeting crime on the southeast side of the city by giving males ages 14 to 25 another Saturday night option. From 8 to 11 p.m. each week, more than 100 kids gather at the Renaissance Pointe YMCA on Bowser Avenue. Since the program started in February, more than 600 young men have taken part in the program, and there have been absolutely no problems.

Headley says the basketball part of the program targets three W's: When does crime happen? After dark, late at night. Where does it happen? Basically the southeast side. Who is usually involved? Young, black men as either victim or perpetrator.

One night, more than 350 kids showed up to play and watch basketball.

"It energizes you," Headley said. "I'm not the athletic expert, I'm not that guy. I just kind of hang around and meet people, and hang out with kids and crack jokes and stuff."

There's a lot more to it than that, though. There's tireless Renaissance Pointe Executive Director Amos Norman, making sure everything runs efficiently and constantly relating to kids; inspirational speakers telling their life stories; and organizations like The United Way, Ivy Tech, Fort Wayne Community Schools, Lutheran Social Services, the Bloom Project mentoring agency and various employers offering services and sometimes just talking and listening.

"We're all trying to be proactive here, and not wait until something happens," said Derrick Westfield, the Fort Wayne Police Department deputy chief of the southeast quadrant and Fort Wayne United Steering Committee member. "We're putting all of our efforts into this. Our main goal is trying to get to those youth who are on the fence so we can talk to them. If you get to the youth, you have a chance to change things. It's going to make a difference."

Though there's always a need for more, every night there are adults available to talk, mentor and share. Mainly, and maybe most importantly, they pay attention, they invest in these kids.

"It's really a program that galvanizes the entire community around these issues dealing with boys and men of color," said Fort Wayne Boys and Girls Club President and CEO Joe Jordan. "I've been in this work for a long time, and I've never seen an initiative like this, because it brings major stakeholders to the table and people who are system leaders to see how their circle of influence impacts boys and men. It allows people to come together and be potential game-changers for a very vulnerable population in our community."

But Headley, 37, is the heart of it, the person who is great at bringing people together to create an avenue for them to help,

Jordan said.

"There are a lot of people with goodwill in our community who want to help who never had the avenue to do that," Jordan said. "This program provides that with a very good understanding of the problem. Sometimes looking from the distance, you see why something is, but you don't understand it. ... This allows people to come closer and have a better understanding to help in trying to defeat some of these daunting numbers that our boys and men are facing every day.

"Iric has created an environment that is welcoming to everybody. It's powerful to watch."
Headley says it's because now he knows exactly why he went through the things he did as a teenager. He understands the people, the mindset, the challenges, because he survived them. He has a different, hard-earned perspective on life.

"So I now know what those young, black boys are dealing with," he said. "I was the guy who needed that help. I was completely on the wrong side of the line, doing all the worst things. I just had a lot of grace, a lot of mercy, and I didn't get caught. The only advantage I have over them is not money or smarts, but that I have been on both sides of it. They haven't been on this side."

Now he's giving them a chance to maybe see the other side, to have another option.

CHAPTER 45
Adele Mitchell learned to take life in stride
Published Oct. 3, 2002, in The News-Sentinel

Sometimes Adele Mitchell's Concordia Lutheran High School

teammates tease her because she doesn't seem to get nervous before big races. How can that be, they wonder. It's because, in the sophomore's life, a cross country race isn't something to get nervous about.

"I live with my uncle because my mom died when I was 8," she says. "I used to live in Arizona. I've never really known my dad because he abandoned us."

She says this in a matter-of-fact tone as if it's no big deal, which tells something about her assuredness and the strength of her relationship with her uncle. Besides being an assistant volleyball coach at Concordia, Kent Mitchell is a man Adele often refers to as her father.

Adele's mother died from breast cancer while living in Phoenix. Adele came to Fort Wayne, Ind., to live with her uncle and immediately had to adjust.

"I'm not sure who was affected more, me or her," Kent said. "It was an impact on both our lives. It's the best thing that has ever happened in my life.

"God has given me a blessing in bringing her to live with me."

He was 32 when she came to live with him eight years ago.

"I think God knew what he was doing not giving me an infant," he said, laughing.

Early on, Adele thought her uncle was a little nuts when he'd take off on a five-mile run. The former Huntington North High School competitor still runs regularly.

Adele was a sprinter as a seventh-grader when, one day, the coaches asked for volunteers to run the mile.

"I was the last one to be asked, so I really didn't have a choice," she said. "I kind of thought the coaches might think I was cool if I did it when everyone else said no."

Because it was a windy day, the coaches told her to stay behind the lead runner, who was larger. Adele finished five seconds off the school record and often continues to use that strategy.

Now she has evolved into one of the top cross country runners in the state.
She finished 79th in the state meet last year but has one of the state's best times this season.

"She's just a very motivated young lady," Concordia coach Mervin Koehlinger said. "She understands the potential she has and sets her goals to do that."

It has helped to partner with junior Alissa McKaig in practice and during meets. Last year, McKaig won almost every race, and this season, Adele has caught up.

"She's just blossomed and gotten a lot better," McKaig said. "It helps you a lot when you have somebody else in practice who will push you. It makes practice easier for both of us because we can practice together. It's been really fun to grow together this year."

Her uncle also takes an active interest in her running, though he once thought she was going to become a top volleyball player.

"I think it's been really good because he kind of got me to be more competitive," she said. "It was good because I really didn't have a father figure."

Kent says he's extremely proud of her running success. One of the first times he watched her run a distance race, he became very emotional.

"I used to have a real hard time watching her run," he said. "Now, it's just a delight. The neat thing is that she is still herself. She understands she's a pretty good runner, but it's not like she has an ego. It is so much fun."

UPDATE: Mitchell won the state championship as a senior. She is married to former Green Bay Packers player Jeremy Thompson, who is doing his residency at the Mayo Clinic, and they have three children.

CHAPTER 46
Josh Clark shows he's a real superhero
Published Oct. 31, 2017, on News-Sentinel.com

Like a lot of 13-year-old boys, Josh Clark loves superheroes, one in particular.

"I have always liked running because I have loved the thought of having superspeed like The Flash," the Maple Creek Middle School eighth-grader said. "The Flash is supercool, to be able to run at the speed of light and travel at the speed of sound, and it's all in slow motion because everything else is kind of slowed down."

But just like The Flash, Clark has his own superhero origin story that includes experiencing near-death, later overcoming huge obstacles and using what he's learned to help others. He doesn't have a costume, but he does wear a uniform when he runs cross country. He's also got a confidence-inspiring smile and an easy way with people, along with a love of helping others and inspiring them with his acts of goodwill.

Josh was recently named one of eight Riley Hospital for Children champions, a yearlong ambassadorship that involves telling others about your own bravery and committing to motivating others who face medical problems.

What he has overcome and how he uses it to help others is definitely heroic. Basically, he's aspiring to follow his hero's example.

When he was born, Josh weighed 6-pounds, 14 ounces. His strawberry-sized heart had a major problem because his aortic valve was closed, meaning he would die if doctors couldn't open it. If they pushed too far, his valve could have exploded; if they didn't push far enough, it would not have helped at all.

The procedure took two hours, with his parents, Matt and Laura, holding hands and praying in the waiting room for their 1-day-old baby. There was really nothing else they could do.

The catheterization was successful, and he was able to come home after 17 days with the hope of holding off his next surgery until he was 1 year old. But all the surgery did was buy a little time — eight weeks. This time, his aortic valve was replaced with his pulmonary valve, which was replaced with an artificial valve that had not yet received Food and Drug Administration approval.

Doctors said a cadaver valve would have worn out quickly and Josh would not have reached his first birthday, but he was too small for a mechanical valve, which would have required the use of blood thinners throughout his life. There was no other choice.

Doctors also opened his mitral valve, patched a hole in his heart and enlarged the area below his aortic valve. At the time, his parents weren't too sure everything was treatable, but having Riley Hospital and Dr. John Brown so close was a blessing.

"Riley really gave us hope, because anything that needed done for Josh's heart could be done there, and we gave it to God," Laura said. "We had a strong faith before that, but depending on God through all of this has made it stronger. I think He had a hand in it, because Josh's heart defects are rare, and the surgery he needed was rarely done, and to find out that Dr. Brown who was there specialized in it ..."

Despite a few setbacks, Josh finally came home for good after a month, with the admonition that his valves would likely need replaced every 10 years or so, and he'd require yearly trips to Riley for checkups.

So far, he's been lucky enough to push back starting the clock again almost an extra four years.

There were more challenges along the way as Josh used a feeding tube until he was 8 and struggled until last year with cyclic vomiting syndrome, which meant he barfed as many as 10 times a day. He always kept a good attitude.

"Tube feeding always felt like they were just layering brick by brick in my stomach," he said. "It just didn't feel right, but I guess it's what we had to do."

Partly because his stomach was so small, he simply couldn't

and wouldn't eat much. He'd end up collecting Halloween candy for his brother and two sisters, or he'd have to sit at the Thanksgiving table for an hour while everyone else continued eating. He loved watermelon, maybe because there wasn't a lot of substance or calories.

Now, he eats like a typical teenage boy and loves ribs.

But in a way, his medical issues were sort of like his superhero secret identity. To look at him, no one would have known he's special or different unless he told them. Sure, his school friends knew about the feeding tube, but Josh has always been asked to speak about his heart situation during classes, at assemblies or at fundraisers. He has the courage, determination and willingness to try to help others by being the example at these events. Not everyone can do that, and maybe that's his real superpower.

"I wanted to prove everybody wrong, to kind of prove that I'm normal, too, and I can do what you can do," he said. "I usually like a lot of different stuff that everybody else hates."

He loves art, especially drawing, specializing in portraits of Stitch and The Flash, of course. Most kids also hate running, but he wanted to try in the third grade, so he underwent a series of tests at Riley on a treadmill to see if his body could hold up to the physical stress. He scored in the 90th percentile of "normal" kids.

Still, he revels in his uniqueness and feeling different because he says everyone his age is always doing the same things, something his life taught him about five years earlier than most teenagers figure it out. That's part of why he loves running on the cross country team.

"It makes me feel like I've accomplished something big," he said. "Running is never easy, but I've always said that after the first mile, it kind of feels like flying, because you just let go, your muscles are loose, you feel good, the wind is cruising against your face … it's just nice.

"Running is about determination, and there's also the mental ability that you have to keep on going when your mind is saying you should probably rest, and it's telling you that you are tired and go sit down. It's tough and challenging, and I like it that way."

And that's kind of the way he approaches his health issues when he talks to others. Josh cares about people and helping them, because, as his father said, it's just part of his nature. He finds ways to make a difference. Maybe all the kids he sees struggling and fighting through issues at Riley inspire him to do so much more.

He's always finding ways to turn his weakness into a strength and then use that to help others, but isn't that what superheroes do? Don't they face down their flaws, overcome their doubts and let their responses define them?

"It's fun to know you get to help people who really can't help themselves sometimes," Josh said. "I understand what they are going through, and I know what I do helps other people's lives. I've been with a lot of people who have disabilities. We all had something wrong with us, but we wanted to give back to someone else."

What could be more like a superhero than that?

CHAPTER 47
Loss helped Matt Hirsch become a better man
Published Nov. 27, 2017, on News-Sentinel.com

After Woodlan High School's 15-14 loss to Southridge in Saturday's IHSAA Class 2A football championship game — where they fell behind in the final minute — I called a friend to talk about what the Warriors must be feeling. Better than anyone, he intimately understands the unique disappointments the Warriors are living with today as they wonder how they might have changed the outcome.

Because the memory of defeat always lingers far longer than the joy of victory, those questions will last a while. My friend knows they can't be answered, only grown from.

Though he was only 5 feet 11 and 175 pounds, Matt Hirsch was a lineman and kicker on the 1981 Woodlan state finals team that lost the Class A title game to Hamilton Southeastern. After Barry Ehle's state-record 94-yard kickoff return for a touchdown, an extra point was blocked, but Hirsch had a chance to win the game with 11 seconds left on a 33-yard field goal.

"I think I had done everything I could to prepare for that moment," Hirsch said. "I kicked it exactly as I wanted to. I thought it was perfect. Then it was no good."

As the kick sailed wide right by about three feet, Hirsch's head was buried into the Lawrence Central High School field mud. He was inconsolable, unable to look his teammates in the eyes because he had let them down.

He can name them all: Barry Ehle, Devin Anderson, Mike

Hetrick, Jeff Berning, Troy Gerig, Kevin Shull, Billy Smith, Lowell Delagrange, Mike Szajna, Nick James, Todd Brown, Jerry Hammon, Bob Tuggle and Ralph Kurtz were his senior teammates, not to mention Jim and Steve O'Keefe, Mike Kouder, Todd Heckley, Dale Miller, Mitch Armbruster, Brent Werling, Todd Gerbers, Lynn Frecker, Steve Goeglein, Scott Goeglein, Tony Persyn, Keith Delagrange, Mark Kinney, Dave Shanebrook, Gary Vondran, Brian Evilsizer and Bob Doctor.

"These fellas all felt the pang of defeat as I did," Hirsch said. "They understand how this group of boys feels today. When you have a chance to win it for your team, your coaches, your school and your community … it just hurts. I had to deal with some adversity, I had to figure out what was important."

In some ways, the miss haunted Hirsch, but mostly he buried it far inside and tried not to think about it. He decided to continue playing football and attended Valparaiso University, where his freshman roommate already knew what happened. There were a few nights we stayed up talking about it — and he's always been there for me when I needed him to listen.

But what makes me the proudest about being Matt Hirsch's friend is that he never allowed that miss to define him or determine what kind of man he was going to become. It certainly affected him, and sure, he has regrets and it still hurts, but mostly it drove him to be a better person, believer, teacher, coach, husband and father. He fought past it, and it was a struggle.

"Sure, sometimes I wonder what my life might have been like, but I believe I'm far richer today because I missed it," he said. "Would I be a teacher today? Who knows. I wondered what happened to the boys on the Hamilton Southeastern team. How did their success propel them forward? My failure inspired me forward."

After starting his college career believing he wanted to become an engineer, Hirsch changed his major and found his true calling as a teacher, first in Indiana (he coached at Woodlan from 1983 to 1999) and then in Michigan, Florida and now back in Michigan at South Pointe Scholars, a charter school in Ypsilanti.

"Learning how to prioritize is what truly is important," Hirsch said. "I think I have a little bit of a different bent than most people when it comes to athletics. Winning was important and it would drive me nuts if we lost, but I think what I shared with every senior I coached after their last game was a hug and an 'I love you.' It was about the relationship, the people, the connection. Wins and losses ultimately didn't matter. What mattered to me was how was I a part of this journey with you? Did I help you become a better man, a stronger person?"

Those memories built together on the field, the court or on the mats are the most important things that last, which shape the young men and women into what they will become. Scores don't last as long as people, and frankly, they never should. There are always more important things ahead such as parenting, family and friends.

"I think I am far richer, a better person, a better Christian and a better everything having missed that field goal," he said. "I sure would have liked to have made it and seen what else would have happened, but again, where would I be today?"

So many friends and family members told Hirsh over the past two weeks they hoped the Warriors would win the state title for his sake. He simply hoped they'd win for themselves.

But Hirsch knows exactly how the Warriors feel today, and his heart hurts for them. He knows it's going to take time to recover and heal, but he also knows that with strong guidance they will.

As he was driving home last night, a thought from a Lutheran school teacher came back to him. "Winning doesn't make you a champion, it's what you do with experiences that ultimately determine a champion."

CHAPTER 48
Friends and faith help Kevan Chandler live life
Published Oct. 16, 2017, on News-Sentinel.com

Because of spinal muscular atrophy, Fort Wayne's Kevan Chandler may be confined to a wheelchair, but thanks to his friends, he is certainly not limited to one.

Though the messages from his brain to his spinal cord are garbled and cause his limbs to atrophy, Chandler, 31, has an amazing core of friends in North Carolina and Indiana who help him live life. He met many of them while working in the music industry as a harmonica player and podcast editor, and they all take part in caring for his needs. It's an accepted part of who he is, so much so that his friends don't consider it as requiring extra effort. They figure out how things can work in different ways because he's simply part of the group, and that's naturally what they do. He's not a burden but a blessing.

As one of his buddies said, "When you have a dream, everybody understands teamwork makes the dream work."

But around mid-June 2015, Chandler came up with something that would test them all: a tour of Europe without his wheelchair. A wheelchair would anchor them and limit their opportunities, and instead, he would ride along in a backpack. The first gut reaction from everyone should have been, "That's a great idea, but …" There were a few of those, of course, but the main reaction was, "How can we make this work?"

"We didn't know if it would really happen until we were on the plane," Chandler said. "We were waiting for the other shoe to drop. There were plenty of moments where we were kind of worried."

But they never lost faith, which plays a tremendous part in their story. First, they had to figure out how to physically make the situation work. Chandler and his buddies redesigned a Deuter backpack, which was designed to carry a toddler up to 48 pounds. Chandler weighs 65 pounds. The backpack had to be reinforced, recovered in hammock material and tested in various ways. The seat had to be designed so he could be comfortable but also sit high enough with a neck support to see over the head of the person carrying him. He also had to be stable enough to help the person carrying him maintain balance.

Then they had to raise the money for the trip — approximately $35,000 for seven men — and started a GoFundMe page. Things were a little slow until the effort started receiving media attention that spread nationally. As social media reached out, a family in England offered to host them, and they started a nonprofit foundation "We Carry Kevan," which has approximately 37,000 likes on Facebook. Dozens of families facing similar challenges wrote in to ask how the fundamentals of the process would work.

Momentum was on their side, helping push things forward.

"I was utterly surprised and blown away with every success

we had," said Tom Troyer, a singer and songwriter from Greensboro, N.C. "I didn't want to say no, but there were so many conversations where I was shaking my head talking to the other guys and saying, 'This is very unlikely to happen.'

"Kevan has really helped me to see in ways that he does. He has shown me that God does quite a lot through unsuspecting people and surprises us quite often. Kevan's faith touches so many people."

The trip worked perfectly. They spent a week in France, England and Ireland. Ben Duvall, Philip Keller, Robbie Barnes and Troyer were the muscle carrying Chandler, while Luke Thompson and Jamison Hill were the filmmakers who chronicled everything for a documentary. The carriers would serve for 45 minutes to an hour at a time, taking every fourth day off when they could do anything they liked, including leaving the group. A second backpack taken as a precaution was never needed.

"My thing with traveling is I'm not a tourist," Chandler said. "I don't necessarily want to see this famous site and that famous site. I don't like just passing through a place to say I've been there. I want to settle in. We went to all these places because I wanted to be a part of them. We weren't just going to pass through."

He wanted to become part of the places he was seeing, not change them. Some of the areas would have been inaccessible to a wheelchair, but the backpack allowed him to experience the atmosphere.

The only injury had nothing to do with a sore back or pulled leg muscle. While riding in a car, the driver had to stand on the brakes to avoid an accident, and Chandler suffered a broken nose when he jerked forward.

The group anchored in Paris for a week and took off each day to explore. During a stop in London, they asked for help exchanging currency and then had to explain their trek.

"We watched them go from happy-go-lucky to tearing up," Troyer said. "It was really cool to have the opportunity to see others be inspired by what we were doing. Everywhere we went, people went out of their way to help us."

Maybe ironically, the friends don't consider that they were helping Chandler fulfill his dream as much as he figured out a way to take them along. This wasn't a sacrifice for them, but a natural exploration of their friendship, an opportunity to bond even closer as a family of people. Chandler just has a knack of making things work for himself and others.

If anything, he was more dependent upon his friends along the trip than normal because he didn't have his wheelchair.

"We just figured it out," Troyer said. "We just went for it. All the best things just happened, and it really has impacted our faith to understand that God provides."

And he's still providing, as Chandler sees it. He's writing one book, planning another, running the website http:// wecarrykevan.com and working on a documentary about the trip.

The We Carry Kevan foundation has provided so many opportunities to speak and inspire others (taking his friends along) that since July, he's only been home in Fort Wayne, Ind., for about two weeks. Hundreds of people and families have reached out to ask about backpacks. Before the trip, he was a podcast editor; since then, he's been trying to find time to fit that work in. Now he has plans to travel and speak all over the world.

"I can see how the Lord has developed my life to be what it is, which is inspiring and building people up, bringing people together and challenging the status quo of disability," he said. "And saying no, this isn't what it has to look like. Let's think outside the chair and outside the box! I can definitely see how the Lord put that together in my life."

His entire life has become about proving that with friends and faith, there are no limitations.

CHAPTER 49
Komets rally around athletic trainer's daughter
Published Jan. 23, 2018, on News-Sentinel.com

With a smile that lights up her eyes and a giggle that is a gift from God, 4-year-old Makayla Willett has some of Fort Wayne's toughest and strongest athletes willing to do just about anything for her. She also might be more resilient than all of them.

Makayla's dad is Fort Wayne Komets athletic trainer Matt Willett, so she's around the rink and the team frequently, but one place the players never expected to find her was at Lutheran Children's Hospital. When the team made their recent annual Christmas visit, Makayla and her mom and dad were there for what to them has become a normal, weekly visit, but it's something that would terrify most parents.

Makayla deals with idiopathic thrombocytopenic purpura (ITP), a disease that afflicts between 4.3 and 5.3 kids per 100,000 and limits her production of platelets, which are critical to clotting to stop bleeding. A normal count is 150,000 to 450,000, but Makayla's counts have bounced between as low as 4,000 and as high as 73,000.

There's no consistency, so she suffers horrific bruises. If she runs into the corner of a couch, instead of a normal 7-to-10-day window for a bruise, she'll have a deep, dark bruise for at least three weeks, and simple wounds like a paper cut or a hangnail can be serious challenges.

"A normal cut that would take 30 seconds to stop on any child could take 5 to 10 minutes for her," Matt Willett said. "When you go for a blood draw, the puncture wound bleeds for 10 minutes and instantly bruises, when in most kids you never even see the stick point. She smashed her finger between a chair and a table at school, and her finger turned completely black."

At times, medical personnel have questioned possible abuse until the parents have explained their situation.

The biggest worry is that she somehow suffers a head wound, because that could require an emergency room visit. A bloody nose was once a 10-minute affair.

"This is just the roller coaster we get to ride," Jenny Willett said calmly. "It's normal for us at this point."

No one knows the cause, though the Willetts have heard four or five possibilities from doctors who are sometimes educating themselves about the disease as much as they are. It's not thought to be hereditary or genetic, but Makayla's parents have searched their own medical records and memories to see if there were any similar incidents when they were children.

One of Makayla's unique factors is that she didn't experience any symptoms until she was 3 years old when a lab test in August 2016 showed her platelets had dropped to 11,000. An infusion pushed them back to 32,000, and the week after that, the numbers went to 271,000, but then they dropped back to 113,000 then 96,000 then 45,000. By December, they had rebounded to 132,000, but by March 2017, they had dropped again to 36,000. Recently, they were recorded at 73,000, but last week they were all over the place again.

The Willetts have a standing lab order at Dupont Hospital in Fort Wayne, Ind., for weekly blood draws to check Makayla's platelet count. Her current treatment consists of weekly injections, which the Willetts do themselves at home. There are nearly daily calls to the office of Dr. Lubua Ahmed at Lutheran Children's Hospital to check lab results, adjust the injection dosage or ask for advice. Since August, Makayla and her parents have visited the doctor's office 15 times.

Makayla knows the routine so well, she's usually ahead of the procedures, such as pulling up her hair so her ears can be checked. Last week was a rough one, but she powered through as if getting poked and taking infusions were normal.

"She's been to more doctor's appointments in four years than I have in 34," Matt Willett said. "I can't even count how many doctor's visits she's been to.

"A lot of it is if mom and dad freak out about it, she freaks out about it. Jenny and I have to maintain as much calm as possible. As much as we want to cry, throw things and get mad, you have to maintain a level head."

But that must be impossible. How do you try to protect a 4-year-old with the usual incredible energy and invulnerable attitude? There's no cocoon to place her in, no way to avoid everything that can happen.

So the Willetts have chosen to let Makayla experience life as normally as possible, trusting in their faith that God will protect her and guide them. As they see it, it's really their only option.

"We're beyond questioning, 'God, why are you doing this to us?'" Matt Willett said. "We're at the point now that it has brought us closer in our faith and in our family, and now it's about how can our faith help us in the healing process as well? You trust that God is going to get you through these challenges. That's what we're trying to teach her."

And they rely on friends to give them a boost, such as the Komets, who have been very supportive. The players all know the situation and continually ask Willett for updates. Makayla's favorite player is Cody Sol, who always responds to her with a high five. When she was told the guys would be at the hospital for the Christmas visit at the same time, her eyes just lit up.

"The guys are absolutely amazing," Jenny Willett said.

"She just eats it up," Matt Willett said. "She's got them all wrapped around her little finger. To have the support and the understanding from your employer or (those) who you work with the most helps tremendously. For being how much I'm not home, they understand that the time we do get with our families is precious."

Both the Willetts grew up in Huntington, Ind., and the proximity to both of their families was a big reason why Matt took the Komets job last summer. They've needed every ounce of that support and know they will likely need more.

"We don't want her to feel like she's different than anybody," Matt Willett said. "We want her to have as normal enough childhood (as) she can despite this."

And those smiles and the giggles make everything worth it.

CHAPTER 50
Maverick meets the Mad Ants
Published March 18, 2018, on News-Sentinel.com

What if you knew your child was soon going to die, and there was nothing you could do?

After exhausting all medical options, would you beg God for a miracle or scream at Him in rage? Would you fold into yourself and your bed, or could you fight your way through despair's crushing embrace? No matter how desperately you wanted to do something for this child, could you find acceptance in your helplessness? While trying to make every day as good as possible for this child, could you find a way out of the horror and into a hint of a new purpose?

Could you hold onto this child and find the strength from that grip to look ahead?

John and Jessica Weimer are trying to do everything they can for their son, 4-year-old Maverick, who has leukodystrophy, an incurable brain disorder. It's likely he won't live past age 10. They know this, and there's nothing they can do.

Despite examining him since he was five months old, doctors needed 3 1/2 years to diagnose the disease last August, and his parents can describe that day exactly — what the weather was, where they parked the car and how many chairs were around the table as the geneticist explained. They recognized early on they were most likely up against something that had no cure and were prepared to make any sacrifice the rest of their lives, but they didn't dream it was terminal. For 3 1/2 years, they thought if they just prayed hard enough, worked hard enough with various therapies and consulted enough doctors, they could make Maverick's life better, livable.
But they could not.

Leukodystrophy affects one in every 7,600 children, and Maverick's strain is even rarer. It is degenerative and progressive, meaning the symptoms keep getting worse at a continually quicker rate. He will first lose the ability to swallow, and protecting his airway will be increasingly critical. If Maverick lives long enough, he won't be able to hear or see, and he's already lost the ability to crawl or talk. While his 8-year-old sister and 6-year-old brother run and play, Maverick gets frustrated because he cannot.

But he can love now, and he can pop wheelchair wheelies at will as he showed the Fort Wayne Mad Ants basketball team after Friday's pregame shootout while his father told his story. John Weimer will tell anyone he can, because that has become his purpose out of this. Unless God decides otherwise, John can't help his son, but he's hoping to help someone else's child by informing and raising awareness.

He compares the disease to amyotrophic lateral sclerosis (ALS), but leukodystrophy — though it affects far more people — hasn't had a Lou Gehrig, Stephen Hawking or Ice Bucket

Challenge to call attention to it. This has become Maverick's parents' mission.

They are focused, motivated, determined. They recently moved back to Indiana from Wisconsin for John Weimer's job as executive director of sales operations of Aunt Millie's Bakeries. That put them closer to family. It also gave them a new audience.

In a way, their story is about Maverick, but it's also no longer about him. It's possible that he may die any day and likely it will happen by age 8, but maybe they can use that time to reach out, to influence people and to ask others to help them fight this disease. Maybe Maverick can be the spark that leads to a cause that finds the cure. Maybe he can live on in a way that would be incredibly meaningful to others.

Maybe this is the way his parents cope, though that word is so incredibly insufficient. This is their motivation through this, something not to distract them but to channel their emotions, to give purpose to their pain so it isn't entirely hopeless.

Two weeks ago, John gave the sermon at Brighton Chapel in Howe, Ind., and talked about Genesis 22, the story of Abraham and Isaac. God had a purpose with that impossible test. It also foreshadowed Lent and Easter and the life and death of Jesus, John said. What if Maverick's struggles could lead to something greater just like those stories, he asked?

As a dad and a former athlete, it's ingrained in John to fix things, to keep fighting, to overcome challenges by continuing to work at them. He is compelled to do something, anything. There must be a higher purpose from Maverick's life and struggle — there just has to be! Anything else is unacceptable, unthinkable.

His parents are holding onto their faith and the knowledge that they will eventually see Maverick again someday in heaven, where he'll be running and jumping and talking, and he'll be able to hug them back, and physically and vocally express his love for them. They tell him they love him all the time now, but they also are trying to do something else to show it by inspiring others with Maverick's story.

If anything constructive can come from Maverick's struggle and their lives, they are going to find it. They can't and won't give up on that, because that goal can give definition to these few years of his life. Maybe, they think, this is what God has planned for us out of this. Maybe this is the higher purpose.

Medicine may say this is a lost cause, but what if their struggle creates another cause they can win?

CHAPTER 51
Cami Wood is thriving despite losing leg
Published June 21, 2018, on News-Sentinel.com

This winter, Evan and Lisa Wood faced a decision that would affect the rest of their daughter's life. Cami was born with a developmental disorder called melorheostosis, which meant her left leg wasn't developing and had pulled her kneecap to the inside of her leg.

Their two options were a series of five or six surgeries over the next six to eight years with a 15 percent chance of success, or an amputation and the use of a prosthetic leg the rest of Cami's life. After getting two second opinions, the Woods sat the 7-year-old down and explained the possibilities.

"She thought about it for a couple of weeks, and she said,

'Mom, I've made my decision,'" Lisa Wood said. "I got a little anxious, but she said, 'I want to get a new leg to be faster and be able to beat Coach Davidson.'"

Blackhawk Christian School boys basketball coach Marc Davidson was also Cami's physical education teacher, and somehow the topic of who is faster came up.

"He thought he was going to be faster than me, so I said, 'Let's have a race!'" Cami said.

That race this upcoming school year has been her main motivation during therapy, and nobody seems to like Davidson's chances much.

"My guess is she's going to beat me," Davidson said. "She's got a ton of spunk."

Cami's other motivation was to have the surgery completed in time to acquire her prosthetic so she could play Wildcat Baseball this summer. She had the surgery in February, and three weeks ago, she received her prosthetic, just in time for the season. She's just learning how to use her new leg, but she loves playing first base and proudly wears shorts to display her new leg.

"It was a hard decision," she said. "This year, it's hard running, but once I get into the season more, it will probably get easier."

It's doubtful her parents or coaches could have stopped her from playing anyway. A month after her surgery, Cami was hopping all over the basketball court to celebrate Blackhawk Christian's boys basketball regional victory. When her parents tried to explain she couldn't participate in Davidson's basketball camp, the coach invited her to help out as scorekeeper. Before Davidson could turn around, Cami was on the court doing most of the dribbling drills — on one leg.

"The first day she came back to gym class, I wasn't sure how she was going to respond and thought that was going to be a tough day for her," Davidson said. "The other kids were doing warm-ups and running stuff, and she was right down there on the gym floor cheering on her friends and classmates. I was getting choked up just watching her. I could tell right off the bat there was going to be no feeling sorry for herself. I expect her to do amazing things in her life."

Her personality is already amazing, full of life and giggles, unending determination and a little bit of attitude, and as her father said, happy-go-lucky like she has the world by the tail.

"She's the only one of my (four) kids who could have handled this," Evan Wood said. "She has the right personality to be able to attack this full force. God was no dummy when he picked her. He knew what He was doing and who He was picking."

One day last week, Wildcat coach Mark Mugg called her "Woodsy." A few days ago, he called her Cami, and she responded, 'My name's not Cami, it's Woodsy! Call me Woodsy.'"

"Her personality is so infectious, you can't walk away from her without having a great feeling," Mugg said. "Her perspective is incredible, and her smile is everything."

As her mother said, sometimes her folks have to look away and just allow Cami to try something, because she's probably going to do it anyway. She'll also likely succeed. Her orneriness is a good thing for the most part, and her therapist said Cami is already months ahead of schedule. After surgery, her biggest question was whether she could take her leg off and kick her brother with it by swinging it at him.

Her baseball teammates no longer look at her prosthetic. To them, she's just Cami. Eventually, she said she wants to become a Wildcat coach.

"She's what Wildcat was designed for, where everybody makes the team," said St. Joe Wildcat Co-Director Mark Koos. "This program allows her to flourish and show off her abilities."

Someday, Cami hopes to play volleyball and tennis at Blackhawk Christian, but she also likes gymnastics. No one else would be surprised if she ended up on the softball team as a first baseman or catcher. A year from now, she'll be able to test out her first prosthetic leg designed for sports.

"The things you learn watching her are that the things you think are limits are not limits," Evan Wood said. "In Cami's mind, she's not behind, she's still going to win. It's pretty cool to be inspired by your daughter, because it literally does not faze her."

Sounds like Davidson had better start training a little harder.

CHAPTER 52
North Manchester rallies around miracle baby
Published June 13, 2018, on News-Sentinel.com

A couple of months ago, Kara Terflinger and her daughters were in the grocery store when a woman walked up to look and coo at 6-month-old baby Finley. At first, the woman was baffled why the baby looked so familiar.

"Wait a minute!" she finally exclaimed. "Is that Finley? Finley Fierce! I follow her on Facebook!"

Lots of people want to believe in miracles, but have they ever actually seen one? There are about 6,000 people in North Manchester, Ind., who are helping one happen.

When Finley Terflinger was born Sept. 14, 2017, her parents Tim and Kara drove to the hospital in 18 minutes, and she arrived almost as quickly, less than 30 minutes after they walked in the door. That's been about the only easy part of her or their lives since. They named her Finley Sloane because both mean "warrior," but they had no idea she would fight so hard to live up to the names.

They came home after one day, but whenever Kara would nurse, sweat beads would pop up all over Finley's head. She also would suck and suck, but half the milk always spilled out of her mouth.

"She had this smell," Kara said, "and I know how weird it sounds, but she smelled like disease."

"She was always warm when she was sleeping," Tim said. "When she would eat, when she got done, it sounded like she had to cough to clear her throat, and that never went away."

Kara, the mom of a son and four girls (Nicholas, 16; Trinity, 13; Avery, 10; Maggie, 9; and Remington, 2) before Finley, brought her concerns to the pediatrician a week later, and the doctor suggested that Finley was a hot sleeper and that her throat problem was likely laryngomalacia, a partial airway obstruction of which 90 percent eventually disappear. An appointment with an ear, nose and throat specialist was set for February, but then everyone in the family got sick around Christmas.

As Kara was checking everyone's temperatures, Finley's was highest, about 102 degrees.

Another trip to the doctor suggested an ear infection, the first of three in a row requiring 10-day antibiotic prescriptions. Somehow, Finley maintained her weight and matched the growth charts, but then she spiked a 105-degree temperature and bloodwork tests started.

Three days later, the results showed a blast cell that can be a precursor to acute myeloid leukemia (AML), a cancer. It can also be a false positive, so more tests were ordered, and Finley was sent to Lutheran Hospital in Fort Wayne, Ind., for a 48-hour observation. That night, she didn't have a fever and the bloodwork and chest x-ray came back negative, so she was sent home after 24 hours.

Next, she was sent to an infectious disease specialist and then back to a cardiologist for more x-rays, which found fluid around Finley's heart. She was moved to Riley's Children's Hospital in Indianapolis on Jan. 25, and that's when doctors told the Terflingers there was a 6-centimeter by 6-centimeter tumor in Finley's chest putting pressure on her airway. The fluid around her heart was leaking from the tumor.

At first, doctors weren't sure if it was AML or Langerhans cell histiocytosis (LCH), which is another rare cancer from abnormal blood cells produced by bone marrow. AML often produces LCH markers and vice versa, though its treatment is less aggressive than AML, meaning more tests. Eventually, genetic testing was ordered when doctors disagreed on the diagnosis.

The Terflingers were sent home Feb. 10, but Finley got sick again on Feb. 14, meaning another ambulance back to Lutheran and then another to Riley the next day. During her ride to Indianapolis, her heart rate was 260 and her temperature rose from 99 to 104 degrees in a half hour. While waiting for the genetic testing results, she spent 21 of February's 28 days at Riley, scaring her parents to death.

"Everything was, 'What if? What if? What if?'" Kara said.

Throughout, Finley has always been a smiling, happy baby. She didn't know she was sick and loved being picked up and spoiled by her sisters and grandparents.

Inspired by a "Finley the Fighter" Facebook page designed by Kara's cousin Katie Jo Lemming, everyone in North Manchester followed along and kept praying.

"I strongly believe that we've gotten through 100 percent of what we have by posting what's going on with her and knowing that all of those people (were) praying for her," Kara said.

This was especially true after the genetic testing came back as LCH, the lesser of the two possibilities because chemotherapy for that treatment is much less severe. Finley never lost any weight or hair. The prescribed treatment was weekly for seven weeks, followed by every three weeks up to a year.

"That was a God thing," Tim said.

Except that's when the real miracle happened. After the first seven weeks of treatment, scans showed the tumor had disappeared.

Throughout all of these trials, the North Manchester community has stepped up to help. Meals were left for the older kids, Congregational Christian Church hosted a "Finley Fierce Day," the American Legion Post 286 hosted a dinner and concert, hair stylists donated to an auction, motivational bracelets and "Finley Fierce" T-shirts went on sale, a motorcycle club held a ride and money was donated to pay the family's bills. There has been plenty of anonymous help, and Tim's employers at Midwest Poultry have provided constant support.

"There's not enough 'Thank yous' to … not a way to …" Kara said. "It's still overwhelming seeing people post spring break pictures from all over the country wearing her shirts."

There are so many little episodes of help that have added to this run of blessings that the Terflingers don't know how they can possibly say "thank you," but they are going to try. They will host Finley's first birthday party in September at Art's Country Park, and they are inviting the community. Along with celebrating Finley, they'll celebrate the town that continues to help them pull through.

Throughout the continual tests, the Terflingers' faith continues to grow.

"When you go to church and hear stories about this or that happening, you never think that could happen to your family," Kara said. "You have faith and believe that happened for them, awesome for them, but it wasn't firsthand for you. When it's firsthand, it's like, 'Wow!'"

Finley is still fighting every day, usually to stay awake. Because she's on steroids, she's constantly restless and has slept through the night twice in eight months. She's always active, always moving until she crashes, but only sleeps for so long before scooting again, still always happy. Even now when she's lifted or put down, her little legs pump as if she's a sprinter anxious to take off.

There may be more medical challenges, but she's going to have an amazing life.

"I believe God has great plans for her life," Kara said, "and she's going to do great things."

CHAPTER 53
Step by step, Alissa Jagger reached her goal
Published June 12, 2018, on News-Sentinel.com

Ever seen the Christian poem "Footprints in the Sand"?

One version starts with the verse:
"I was walking along the beach with my Lord. Across the dark sky flashed scenes from my life. For each scene, I noticed two sets of footprints in the sand, one belonging to me and one to my Lord."

The next two verses talk about the toughest times during the person's life, and then they notice only one set of footprints in the sand. The final verse concludes:

"He whispered, 'My precious child, I love you and will never leave you, never, ever, during your trials and testings. When you saw only one set of footprints, It was then that I carried you.'"

She may not have realized it as she walked across the stage Friday night to receive her Columbia City (Indiana) High School diploma, but Alissa Jagger probably would have found one set of footprints if she had taken the time to look down. Instead, she was only looking ahead as her smile showed the joy of completing her three-year goal.

During a July 17, 2015, auto accident in Beckley, W.V., Jagger suffered the worst injury of her four family members present in the vehicle: a dislocated spine that paralyzed her from the waist down. Doctors never told her she wouldn't walk, but the damage was so complete that there was nothing to suggest a hint of hope to even discuss.

Still, Jagger never gave up her determination to walk, or her faith to lead her to do it. Sure, medical science may say it was impossible, but …

"God doesn't give you stipulations about when you should live for Him, like if you have a spinal cord injury, or you aren't feeling well or if you have cancer, then you don't have to be joyful or live with the fruits of the spirit," she said. "There's no stipulation on that; whatever happens in your life, too bad, you still have to praise God."

In fact, there are a few dozen examples along her three-year journey to graduation where Jagger and her family can point to what they say was God's guiding hand. Minutes after a car turned into their lane to make an illegal U-turn while they were driving 76 mph on their way to a vacation in Virginia Beach, Va., the miracles started happening.

The accident was so bad, Jagger's dazed brother Cam asked his father, Chad, if this was a dream, but somehow they all survived — a statistical impossibility — as did the other car's three passengers. Two EMTs were driving by and stopped to help, including one with the name John Meracle, who had retired to become an actor.

While the Jaggers recuperated in Charleston, W.V., the Columbia City community rallied with gifts and visits, constant encouragement and even private plane rides.

Everyone kept praying. There may not have been enough money for everything, but someone was always there to help with a donation or time. A woman from North Carolina saw Amy Jagger struggling to walk to the laundry room and insisted she would take care of it. Long after the insurance company informed the family the payments were ending, they found ways to persevere.

"There are so many ways God was there to help us with things," Chad Jagger said.

A former excellent cross country runner, her family believes Alissa is so mentally tough (what they really mean is bull-headed) that when she needed to use special toothpaste, the joke was, "Well, at least you are sensitive about something." It's not that she is especially blunt or unfeeling, but she's straight-forward in her beliefs, expectations and understanding of her capabilities. She holds a lot of her emotions inside as fuel, continually demands more of herself and always keeps driving until accomplishing her goal.

She never gave up on walking at graduation. It wouldn't be a normal walk, but it would be going across the stage on her feet in some form.

"I didn't quite understand everything that was wrong with me," she said. "I said everything else in life depends on how hard you are willing to work at it, so I thought I'd be walking eventually.

This shouldn't be a big deal, I'll be back in no time."

The surgery to stabilize her back took seven hours and required a plate, two steel rods and 12 screws. She recovered in Charleston for 10 days before transferring to Shepherd Center in Atlanta, where she learned to use her new body and a wheelchair. On June 16, 2016, with the help of braces, a walker, a safety belt and a therapist, she stood for the first time. After that, every day off from school was spent in a Chicago clinic pushing for more.

She's been working three years with the goal of walking to receive her diploma, but the culmination wasn't about how far Jagger has come but more about where she plans to go.

"I try to look into the future," she said. "I think that's the only way you can keep your sanity in a situation like this. If you only look back at the past, you can't change that. You can't change the future if all you are doing is looking back. The community is still with me three years later, and they will care about me and what's going to happen. They haven't given up on me."

Jagger said she really didn't expect anything during her walk across the stage because the audience was asked to hold their applause until the end, but everyone started clapping before Jagger stood from her wheelchair, and eventually, everyone in the gym was standing. The applause lasted for more than a minute.

Even Miss Bull-headed (oops, we mean mentally strong) almost started crying, overwhelmed by the goodness of the community and all the people who continue pulling for her.

"It freaks people out, because when she takes a step, she can't feel her foot hitting the ground," her mother said. "It's literally a step of faith every time she walks."

There are still people who doubt and ask if she can actually walk. Some others wonder if she just wanted the attention. They didn't get to see the leg braces under her robe or pay much attention to the walker she used.

There also are others who say they still believe someday she'll walk without the braces or the walker. Right now, she's focusing on attending Grace College in Winona Lake, Ind., and double-majoring in finance and communications. She doesn't know that she'll walk again, but she also doesn't know that she won't. That part isn't up to her.

"That's another reason I have to stay in shape," she said. "For me, it's about showing the Lord's goodness as much as I can, Him through me. It's kind of crazy to think of all the ways God has worked in my life through all of this, all these opportunities I would not have had if I had been able-bodied, all of those chances God opened up for me and my family.

"People don't need to be afraid. I'm fine. It's all good, and I'm proving it's OK. There's a plan, and it's not all over for me. I can live a productive life, and your body is just a home for your soul, and that's what matters most."

There will still be more challenges, but Jagger and her family are ready for them. This story doesn't end with her walking across the graduation stage.

"So many people told us, 'God's not going to give you more than you can handle,'" Amy Jagger said. "That's not true. It's not Biblical. God does give you more than you can handle, because if I think I can handle it, I'll try to do it all by myself."

Maybe the real message is that they actually can handle anything, but only with God's help, even a long walk across the sand.

CHAPTER 54
Brown family changes their world

During the spring of 2010, Aaron and Erica Brown and daughters Kelsi and MaKenna visited Freimann Square in Fort Wayne, Ind., so Erica could photograph the girls. But there was a homeless man sitting in a corner of the park.

"The whole time we were there, I knew where he was," Aaron Brown said. "I kept looking over my shoulder, because I had this fear that he could rob us and he could hurt my kids."

About a year later, Aaron suggested to his family that they begin volunteering to help others. The Browns were a typical Caucasian, middle-class family who lived on Fort Wayne's southwest side. They were Christians who sensed a calling to get more involved in and give more to the lives of others.

They started on at Tuesday night, joining with Saints on the Streets, a group that would be handing out food and supplies to Fort Wayne's homeless starting at 10 p.m. The girls, who were 9 and 12 at the time, were left at home because Aaron and Erica had no idea what dangers might be present.

One of the people they met that night was the homeless man who had been sitting in the Freimann Square corner.

"He shared his story about how he had been married and his

wife got cancer, and she got sick and passed away, and he didn't take it well and he turned to the bottle," Aaron said. "He had a job in a factory and a home, and he lost all of it. He even lost his kids because he just went in a downward spiral."

The night and the man's story was a shocking uppercut for the Browns, forcing them to admit and face their stereotypes, their preconceptions.

"It was completely eye-opening," Erica said. "You think they're bums and they are lazy and they are not trying, but they actually all have a story. Someone chose to be homeless because his family members were addicts, and if he stayed at home, he would be exposed to it, so he chose to stay clean and be on the streets."

"Walking by on the street, seeing him sleeping on a park bench, the natural reaction was to cast judgment on him," Aaron said. "That whole night was all a reminder to us that we were one life event away. Homelessness does not discriminate. It can happen."

That's how the Browns founded their campaign, which they called Impact 52. The goal was to weekly serve a nonprofit organization in the area. Over the next four years, they volunteered for 208 consecutive weeks with more than 170 nonprofit groups and causes. They even started a blog, Impact52.org, to encourage others with their stories, and there's a list with links to every group and organization they worked with.

Though the girls admit they were reluctant to join in at first, they soon started suggesting places the family could volunteer. By being forced out of their comfort zones, they found their own reasons and purpose.

"I just see life differently," MaKenna said. "I don't judge people on appearances and not knowing their backstory. I used to be really spoiled, and now I have to work for my money and the stuff I've got. I'm a lot more grateful."

Now 17, she volunteers five hours per week as a barista at The Perk Coffee House at Central Ministries Church, which purchases clean water for Africa.

"At the beginning, I was very confused," Kelsi said. "I didn't understand the concept of volunteering. I was satisfied with the life I was currently living. I was stubborn and didn't want change. It took a while to get to the point where I wouldn't complain about having to volunteer. I remember serving at the downtown Fort Wayne Rescue Mission for the first time, and I remember seeing the help that was needed for the community. That was a major turning point in my life. From that day, I have a passion to serve others as much as I can."

The need she saw at the Rescue Mission was a life-changing event for her and made her realize how blessed her life was. When some classmates asked Kelsi why she was volunteering, she said the question they should be asking is why they were not.

"I learned a life lesson with every experience," she said. "I have become more appreciative of the things I have been given. I have learned to not judge others based on what they look like, what they wear. Everyone is struggling with something behind closed doors. I learned what my passion and interests were. Looking back at my experiences as a volunteer, I have learned that volunteering is about giving back to others and expecting nothing in return. I have learned that helping others takes my mind off the stressful areas in my life. My passions of what I want to do with my life involve my community and the communities all over the world. I have learned that I want to change the world in any way that I can."

She's now 20, and one of the reasons she picked her Ball State University sorority was because of its commitment to serve others.

"I learned a lot about being with our kids and being a parent, because going and volunteering makes you a better parent because it shows your kids things that I can't teach them," Aaron said.

Those lessons have stuck as both girls admit they learned more confidence and compassion because of volunteering, and it has changed their perspective on life.
The Browns helped thousands of people over their four years, until their lives changed and it was time for the project to end. The girls were more involved with school, Aaron switched jobs and Erica went back to school. Now the national operations director for Destiny Rescue (which frees children from sexual slavery), Aaron has written three children's books — with plans for 15 more — about the family's experiences.

They learned so much by helping others that they understand they were mainly helping themselves. Aaron never dreamed he could be the main benefactor.

"Obviously, the project changed me as a man and husband and a father," he said. "We were going to church and I was a believer, but I did not have a relationship with God. He called me and brought me closer to Him. To think that I stand in churches today and speak when I wouldn't set foot in a church, I mocked the church, I mocked believers as a young person.

"I can look back on it now and see how He laid the stones out for me to walk to where I am now. He prepared me for the job I have today through the corporate world, through volunteerism. It changed me, but it taught me lessons that I wouldn't have learned other places."

The volunteering was the classroom, and he was the student, Aaron said. There's no doubt who was the teacher, either.

There's one last story from the project's second year that drove home everything God was doing with Aaron. During "Random Act of Kindness Week," Aaron was in a Speedway gas station when he bought coffee for two couples in line behind him. His goal, he wrote on the blog, was to show the week didn't require a lot of time or money to be successful.
Six months later, Aaron ran into the man again at the gas station but didn't recognize him immediately.

"You bought coffee for my wife and me," the man said.

"You're by yourself, where's your wife?" Aaron asked.

"I'm getting ready to go see her. She's in the hospital, she's dying of cancer. Actually, I'm getting ready to take her home for hospice care."

"I'm sorry to hear that."

"I want to thank you again for those coffees."

"You don't have to do that," Aaron said.

"No, you don't understand," the man said. "The day that you bought us that coffee was the day she was diagnosed with terminal cancer. It was the worst day of our life, and you gave us hope that something good could still happen to us. I can't wait to go to the hospital and tell her I saw you."

Afterward, Aaron remembers sitting in his car crying, and now says he's lived his life differently since that day.

"I was asking myself, 'How many moments have I missed because I was so wrapped up in my own stuff that I missed the moment to show somebody that I cared, to acknowledge them?' I still get wrapped up in my world and miss moments, but I try to live differently. Now, I never ask why. What am I a supposed to learn about it to make my life better and the lives of other people better?

"The No. 1 thing that I learned from it all is that we should live our life every day with purpose on purpose," Aaron said. "There are no small gestures. It's not small because it has the power to change a life and make a difference."

ABOUT THE AUTHOR

A lifelong member of Bethlehem Lutheran Church, Blake Sebring has worked in journalism since he was 15 years old, mostly with The News-Sentinel in Fort Wayne, Ind. (1988-2018). "Features in Faith" is his tenth book, including three novels. He was inducted into the Indiana Sportswriters and Sportscasters Hall of Fame in 2015.

Made in the USA
Columbia, SC
16 October 2018